The Disciple Christ Deserves

A Catholic Spiritual Director's Approach

Rev. Michael J. Stalla, DMin

Edited by Marisa Falcione

En Route Books and Media, LLC

Saint Louis, MO

ENROUTE
Make the time

En Route Books and Media, LLC
5705 Rhodes Avenue
Saint Louis, MO 63109

Cover Design: *Pieta,* by Wilhelm Theodor Achterman (1799-1884), Borghese Chapel of the Church of Santissiima Trinità dei Monti, Rome. Photo courtesy of Rev. John Paul Kuzma, OFM Cap.

Illustrations by Sarah Write

ISBN: 979-8-88870-464-6
Library of Congress Control Number:
Available online at https://catalog.loc.gov

Dedication

This book is dedicated to the clergy and religious who most inspired my vocation and discipleship, especially:

Sr. Ann Marie Kanusek, SND,
former principal of Holy Trinity Grade School, Avon.

Fr. Gerard Gonda, OSB,
former principal and president of Benedictine High School, Cleveland.

Fr. John Kline †,
former pastor of St. John Vianney Parish, Mentor.

and

Sr. Rut Noemi Lara, OSC,
former principal of La Academia Católica, Teotepeque, El Salvador.

Table of Contents

Introduction

One of my earliest memories was when I was four or five years old. My grandfather picked me up and placed me on his workbench. Years later I would marvel at the extensive collection of tools he had fastened to the wall and in the drawers. He had the right tool for every job. On this occasion, we were going to build a birdhouse. I am sure I did not help very much. I probably just got in the way. But it was our project that we did together. I was beaming with pride that grandpa wanted me to help. Every Spring, my grandfather and I would check to see if any birds took residence in our birdhouse.

So it is with our Lord, the Creator of heaven and earth. We are invited to participate with the Divine Artisan in the formation of tomorrow. Though I am sure that God could do a perfect job without our assistance, He takes joy in working with His beloved little ones. Working hand in hand with humanity must warm the Sacred Heart, just as it fills us with a sense of purpose, importance, and happiness. It is an honor to be invited to such a noble task!

For us to accomplish this wonderful endeavor, we must follow the same three instructions my grandfather gave to me: Listen to directions, always use the right tool for the specific job, and give it your best effort. In spiritual life, we are talking about **Discernment**. Discernment is not about figuring out good and bad or right and wrong. That is the role of conscience. Discernment is about either recognizing divine communication or choosing between two goods according to God's preference. It is about making a decision together with our Lord.

To learn how to listen to the voice of God, it may be helpful to ask for guidance from a Spiritual Director. I do not believe that everyone always needs a spiritual director. Most of us have the capacity to follow the promptings of our conscience to navigate our daily lives. For some people, by the nature of the work they do or the decisions they have to make, a spiritual director can be very important.

There are **four reasons** why a person might seek spiritual direction. First, for professionals in **pastoral care**, such as priests, religious, deacons, those in formation, other spiritual directors, pastoral ministers, youth ministers, counselors, etc. Because others seek out these professional ministers for guidance, it is essential that they be held to a higher standard of conduct and transparency. With this level of confidence placed in their hands, it is all the more important that they stay honest and focused on the Lord.

The second group of people who look for a spiritual director are those trying to make a **significant decision** in life or trying to interpret something he or she perceived as a prompting of the Holy Spirit. For most people, this occurs periodically when thinking about marriage, children, employment, disruptions in the family harmony, or those mysterious moments in prayer when they get that sneaking suspicion that God is trying to push us toward some next step, especially during those transitions of life such as empty-nesters or retirement. A spiritual director can help them be open to letting God into the decision-making process.

The third group of people that typically asks for spiritual direction is those who are feeling **spiritually lost** or stuck. It is an ambiguous time in their spiritual life. They have lost some of the enthusiasm and confidence they once had in the Lord. They are looking for help to rekindle the fire and the faith they once had.

The last group of people may be looking for a combination of spiritual direction and professional counseling. The two are not the same, but they can be a very powerful means of healing when working in tandem. These are people who have had certain **traumatic experiences** that have affected their relationship with God and others and the way they see themselves. They feel that something is broken and needs to be fixed. They feel trapped by past experiences and are looking for the freedom to move beyond the pain of their personal crosses and into the experience of the Resurrection. This may include anything from being a victim of violence to going through a heart-wrenching breakup. Again, it is important that the person is seeing a professional counselor. Nonetheless, these issues can be both emotional and spiritual in nature. Our Lord sought out just such people to bring them hope, freedom, and healing.

All four types of people who seek spiritual direction are looking for **accountability** in their discipline of faith and progress in their spiritual development, particularly in their relationship with Christ. Of course, there are occasions when a person may want to make an appointment for a single conversation with a spiritual director. However, most of the time, most people would not require a spiritual director but could benefit from an accountability partner or a prayer partner with whom they can contemplate their spiritual lives.

Spiritual direction is distinct from counseling. **Counseling** considers all the factors of a particular decision, issue, or feeling from the perspective of an experienced person who is not directly involved with the situation. For example, a couple that is struggling with communication issues may seek a marriage counselor to help them resolve the latest difficulty. In the process, they hope to recognize the pattern of behavior that causes communication issues and correct it. While a session of spiritual direction may include talking about actual problems in the life of an individual, the conversation is much more focused on prayer and one's relationship with God. Counseling looks for the root cause of issues and corrects them. Spiritual direction pays attention to God's activity and communication in one's life and how to respond to those promptings and revealed truths. Counseling often focuses on the environmental factors that contributed to the development of an individual's personality during their formative years. Spiritual direction aims to reaffirm the identity of the person from the divine perspective. Counseling aims to help people make proper decisions. Spiritual direction aims to help people be in proper relationship with God. The two are related but distinct.

Spiritual direction is not about submitting one's will over to a spiritual director, as if the guru now makes all the decisions of one's life. It is not magic that makes all the difficulties and bad feelings go away. It is not about having the all-knowing teacher give the answers to life's questions, served on a silver platter. It is more like having an interested, experienced friend with whom to mull over the spiritual questions and experiences of one's life.

In our world, there seems to be a shortage of people willing to engage in such conversations. As a result, we are uncomfortable talking to people about what seems so intimate and private. Often, we struggle to find the right words to describe our spiritual life. We fumble with explaining the raw emotions that we feel like we either "should" understand already, or "should not" be feeling at all, such as anger at God or a longing for love.

A session of spiritual direction is a safe place with a confidant who will not judge the person but will attempt to help interpret the spiritual picture that is presented. He or she is a **companion for the journey** toward a deeper relationship with Christ.

Over many sessions, a person receiving spiritual direction will accumulate multiple techniques and spiritual methods of prayer. Each director will have his or her typical method, preferred Saints to draw from, and his or her own style of offering direction. It may be challenging to find available spiritual directors since the demand has grown in recent years. Keep asking for referrals until you find one that is a good fit for your needs.

The first two or three sessions are usually about finding a good fit between the director and the directed. A "good fit" is measured by the ease with which one is able to enter into the depths of conversation about spiritual life with this particular person. Do you feel understood? Are there tangents that distract you from making further progress? Do the advice and insights provided make sense to your experience of life? Do you feel comfortable and confident being honest with your spiritual director?

Once a spiritual director has been established, it is preferable that the directee spends significant time with the same person. Jumping from one director to the next may be an attempt to find someone who simply agrees with one's own perspective. Honest and humble reflection about one's inner motivations is essential to a fruitful spiritual direction relationship. Those who seek spiritual direction desire to progress in their spiritual maturity. Progress is better realized when the spiritual director builds upon past sessions toward a desired goal of development, much like mapping lesson plans in teaching.

However, if you have been with a director for more than a year, you may begin to feel it is time to try another director. Spiritual directors should not take this personally. It should be a decision that is discerned together. The desire for change may be caused by complicated feelings that are not completely understood. Sometimes we grow too close to our spiritual directors. Sometimes we have a basic disagreement that shakes our trust. Sometimes we are at a different stage of life, and we are looking for a different style or level of challenge. Whatever the case may be, make the decision with honesty and humility.

This guide is designed to be a helpful tool for those interested in either receiving or offering spiritual direction. These techniques have been developed over my twenty-two years as a missionary and a diocesan priest. I draw from various spiritual traditions, including Sacred Scripture, the Catechism of the Catholic Church, St. Thérèse of Lisieux, St. Ignatius of Loyola, St. Augustine, St. Paul of Tarsus, St. Teresa of Avila, C. S. Lewis, St. John Paul II's Theology of the Body, Alcoholics Anonymous, the Charismatic Renewal, the Vatican II documents, Stewardship, the Pioneers Abstinence Group, St. Mother Teresa, Our Lady of Guadalupe, my parents and grandparents, and the simple but profound faith of the poor people in El Salvador.

Though I have repackaged a number of ideas in my own words, I was thankful to God to find that the vast majority of the advice I give to people comes from the greater **Church Tradition**, rather than from my own ramblings. You may be familiar with some of the techniques that I suggest within this book. Some may seem like personalized adaptations. Some of the terminologies are changed according to what I consider an easier way to understand the purpose of the tool. Feel free to adapt and rename things as you see fit.

There are various styles of spiritual direction. Some models may not be compatible with other models. In the end, the purpose of spiritual direction is to develop a relationship with Christ. The methods, models, and tools are all secondary to that goal. My loyalty is first and foremost to Christ and His holy mission. I ask my Lord for the humility to let go of the things that are not helpful and embrace the good suggestions of my colleagues.

That being said, I hope and pray that some of these tools are helpful in your ministry and personal development as an authentic disciple of our Lord. Thank you for all that you do to build up God's holy people and for taking seriously the call to be more of the disciple Christ deserves.

Chapter 1

How is Your Prayer Life?

The question that I typically begin any spiritual direction session with is, "How is your prayer life?" It is the central reason why a person is looking for spiritual direction and not counseling. By the nature of the question, it is less about emotions and feelings, and more about evaluating the quality of communication with God.

For most people, they answer the question in one of three ways: 1) "Good, I guess."; 2) "Awfully quiet."; or 3) "I haven't been very disciplined." Even people who have been coming to see me for years typically have some variation of one of these answers. As we begin to pick apart what they mean by their answer, the evaluation begins. People are not accustomed to evaluating their prayer life. It is only in spiritual direction that they ever have a chance to stop and reflect, not exactly about God, and not exactly about themselves, but about how the two are communicating.

The first answer, "Good, I guess," opens up the following questions of how we judge the "goodness" of prayer. Were there specific moments where the communication seemed clear? Were there insights, private revelations, fruits of the Spirit? Is the person simply stating that they have been disciplined in a prayer routine? Perhaps they have not sinned as much as usual? Perhaps they are just feeling happy and at peace?

The second answer, "Awfully quiet," is not a judgment about the quality of prayer. It is more of a recognition that they were expecting or hoping for a clearer dialogue with the Lord. They have not been able to recognize the moments when God has been communicating with them. They are feeling unsure about decisions or the direction of life. They are longing for more euphoric moments that only God can offer. They feel a general discontentment. A good follow up to this response is to ask, "Was there a moment in your prayer life when you were expecting a clearer response? What were you expecting?"

The third answer, "I haven't been very disciplined," is self-centered. The person is under the belief that they are in charge of the conversation. If they have broken their prayer routine, they blame themselves for the lack of communication. They have already determined the culprit and the remedy. They are looking for accountability and motivation. Some good follow-up questions might be, "Why not? Why did you lose your discipline? Did you begin to pray and stop? Did you simply forget, or were you distracted, tempted, or feeling something else? What is life like when you don't pray? Despite your lack of formal prayer, did you encounter God since the last time we met?" The aim is to get the person out of simply thinking he is a bad person and more reflecting on what is happening in and around him when he is struggling with his prayer life.

Prayer does require discipline. **Discipline** requires sacrificing our immediate desires for the sake of our duty. For children, I parallel not talking to God with not talking to your best friend. Even one day seems like a rift in your friendship. For teens, I focus on the way successful people are driven, focused, and disciplined. This is your key to becoming the person you want to be, the person Christ knows you can be. The word, "disciple," is related to the word, "discipline." For adults, I try to get them to understand that temptations are real. They are in the midst of a daily battle for souls. The benefits of prayer far outweigh all the other junk in our lives that will never satisfy us. Imagine what life would be like if you were more dedicated to prayer. Would you look back on judgment day and conclude that a prayerful life was not worth living?[1] Of course not. That is the best way you could live. Envision the goal. Now seek what your heart desires. Do not settle for counterfeit gods!

One of the great excuses people use about not having a formal routine to their prayer life is that they "pray all day long." That is not accurate. They would like to think they do, but that is the point. They think to themselves. Praying is very different than talking to yourself in your mind. We all do it, but it is not prayer. Many times when I am praying, I will drift off to my thoughts and insights. I leave Christ on the sidelines as I play with my imagination. That is not prayer. I

---

[1] Michael Ivens, *Understanding the Spiritual Exercises: A Handbook for Retreat Directors* (Leominster, England: Gracewing, 1998), 143.

have to call myself back to the reality that God is with me. It takes discipline.

Formalized prayers and routines are not for simple-minded people who cannot come up with their own spontaneous prayers. Saints, far greater and smarter than most of us, used these methods for centuries to prevent themselves from drifting off into talking to themselves in their minds. It is worth the effort to break this habit. We can convince ourselves of all kinds of things, and then claim it came from prayer. We must not slap the authority of God on mere personal opinions and whims. It is a mistake that many of us have made and continue to make. Reinterpreting Rene Descartes, "If there is one thing I know for certain, it is that 'I am …not God.'"[2]

IMAGINATION AND PRAYER

The Rosary is an excellent tool that is new for the younger generation. The idea of repeating the same words over and over again is not very appealing to anyone. Yet, when used properly, the Rosary can aid with **Contemplation**. It teaches the basics of the Faith and allows the one praying to explore the depths of the Mysteries with a certain rhythm and safety net. We open up our minds to the Mysteries and spend at least enough time on each of them as it takes to recite the prayers. I say "safety net" referring to the fact that the balance of each mystery prevents our imagination from wandering into heresy. Each mystery steers us back to *the* Truth. Even when they have lost their memories or are actively dying, many people are still

---

[2] René Descartes, *A Discourse on Method*, meditation III.

able to recite the Our Father and the Hail Mary. As I minister to them, I realize that they had prayed the Rosary so often that it becomes the last words on their lips. Have I prayed it sufficiently to make it indelible in my memory?

While we contemplate the mysteries of the Rosary, we open up our **Prayerful Imagination**. We create a mental picture of the scenes of Jesus' Nativity, Passion, or Resurrection. We use our experiences of life to fill in the gaps where the written Word does not adequately describe the events. We imagine colors, sounds, smells, textures, expressions on faces, tones of voices, etc. For Prayerful Imagination to be fruitful, it is best to ask the Holy Spirit to guide your thoughts. This is how the writers of the books of the Bible were inspired by the Holy Spirit. They did not have their eyes roll back in their heads in a trance while their hands scribbled on a page. They wrote what they had experienced in their prayer life. Though they use expressions and imagery from their own times, they are guided by the Holy Spirit to describe a reality that is hard to put into words. This is why each book of the Bible uses various genres.[3] When interpreting the Bible, it is important not to simply find ways to show that the Word of God agrees with you. Instead, pay attention to the way the original audience would have understood the symbols, parables, and metaphors. Just like we use different genres for movies, such as science fiction, fantasy, or history, each book of the Bible is written with a particular literary genre. In the same way, when we pray, it is important to

---

[3] Paul VI, "Dei Verbum," Dogmatic Constitution on Divine Revelation: Dei Verbum, November 18, 1965, https://www.vatican.va/archive/hist_councils/ii_vatican_council/documents/vat-ii_const_19651118_dei-verbum_en.html, chapter III.

open up our imagination to envision, not fiction, but Truth expressed in a way we can understand.

Using Prayerful Imagination, I like to picture the Virgin Mary talking to her relative, Elizabeth. Mary is so excited and talking a mile-a-minute, as do most teenagers. Elizabeth is overjoyed she can share this miracle with Mary. How humble Elizabeth was not to demand attention to be given to herself. After all, her pregnancy is miraculous as well. She was barren but now bears a son. Yet, Elizabeth prefers to focus on Mary. "Blessed are you, Mary."[4] Through this Prayerful Imagination, I begin to feel what each person is experiencing. I have insights into the deeper meaning of their dialogue and the event itself. The Bible becomes more "real" and impactful. These events changed the history of the world! Should they not change me as well?

Prayerful Imaginations can be used to pray through Sacred Scripture, contemplate the Mysteries of the Rosary, or enter into a personal dialogue with the Lord. Again, ask the Holy Spirit to guide your prayer. As we picture Jesus physically with us, the experience changes. We shift from pious platitudes to intimate friendship. We are more capable of letting Jesus communicate to us in words or other means, rather than doing all the talking ourselves. It is a learned technique, meaning we can improve our prayer with practice.

I also use Prayerful Imagination to dialogue with the Saints. Much like the old saying, "*What Would Jesus Do?*," as Catholics, we have a significant number of role models to help us figure out how

---

[4] Luke 1:42 (NAB).

to handle difficult situations well. First, you must study the life or works of a Saint. Next, you ask the Holy Spirit to guide your prayer. Finally, you enter into Prayerful Imagination and try to picture how this Saint would handle whatever situation with which you are confronted. How would St. John Paul II react? What would St. Paul say? If St. Augustine were here, what would be his mode of operation? Try to put on the mind of the Saint and follow through with the reasoning he or she would use. I find St. Thérèse of Lisieux has been my constant companion in my spiritual journey. We talk often in my prayer about applying the Gospel to my life. The more Saints you study, the more diverse the counsel you will have.

I have borrowed the concept of Prayerful Imagination from St. Ignatius of Loyola.[5] It is often connected to contemplation. Ignatius observed that, when he contemplated being a feared warrior on the battlefield, he was filled with enthusiasm and excitement. Afterward, he was left feeling empty. When he was contemplating being like one of the Saints he read about in his books, he was surprised to feel enthusiasm and excitement. The difference was that, afterward, he felt peaceful.[6] He decided that his truest desire, placed there by God, must be to become a Saint. In this way, Prayerful Imagination can help us discover our true wants and desires and the path that leads to our greatest happiness.

---

[5] Ignatius of Loyola, *The Text of the Spiritual Exercises of Saint Ignatius* (London: Burns and Oates, Limited, 1900), 20-21.

[6] Ignatius of Loyola, *The Autobiography of St. Ignatius of Loyola*, ed. John C. Olin, trans. Joseph F. O'Callaghan (New York: Harper & Row, Publishers, Inc., 1974), 23-24.

Another application of Prayerful Imagination is to put on **the Mind of Christ.** How does Jesus view you, others, life, death, pain, sin, virtue, or sacrifice? To know the purpose of the plan of God, in other words to see reality through Christ's eyes, is the gift of Wisdom.[7] Ask the Holy Spirit to impart this gift upon you. What do you see, feel, taste, smell, or hear as you put on Christ? How do you interpret the meaning of the events in your life and the lives of those around you? How deeply does Christ love?

WHAT ABOUT HEAVEN?

Sometimes I use prayerful imagination to contemplate **Heaven itself**, or even the face of Jesus, or the Father in His glory. We claim we want to be with God forever in Paradise. Yet, if our eyes are fixed on worldly goals, do we truly desire what Christ is offering? Or do we just want a perfect earthly existence? Many people find the concept of heaven boring. In heaven, there is no strife or troubles, forever and ever. It sounds like a movie with no point to it. We picture chubby baby angels on clouds playing harps. It just does not sound that appealing. This is because we have a rather immature, uncritical concept of heaven. Spend some real time contemplating the goal and meaning of your life. Ask the Holy Spirit to guide your Prayerful Imagination. We should long for heaven, like a desert longs for water![8]

---

[7] *Catechism of the Catholic Church, Second Edition* (Washington, DC: United States Conference of Catholic Bishops, 2019), glossary, "Wisdom."

[8] Psalms 63:2 (NAB).

Once, I was at the cemetery burying an elderly woman. Her teenage grandson felt comfortable enough to ask me a question when the ceremony was over. He said, "Father, if science and medicine continue to develop at such a high rate, maybe one day there will be a pill that we can take that would prevent us from dying. Then, there would be no more death. If they came up with a pill like that, do you think it would change our faith?" What a great question! I admire his deep thinking and clear focus.

After pausing for a moment to consider his question, I responded with a principle I now call, "**The Immortality Pill**." I said, "Well, if that pill existed, I probably would not take it. You see, my hope is to go to heaven. The passage to heaven is through Christ. 'If we die in Christ, we will live in Christ.'[9] Heaven is a lot different than Earth. On Earth, there is pain and suffering. It is not just physical pain and suffering. There are hurt feelings, misunderstandings, petty fights, and evil inclinations. Besides, life becomes pretty meaningless if we all just scurry around, eating, working, planting, and eating again. Without hope in the reward for following Christ, it all becomes kind of 'vanilla.' While I am here, I intend to do all I can to please the Lord and make my life and the lives of others a little more holy. I have no illusion or hope that we can make Earth into heaven. Yet, maybe we can make it more the Kingdom of God. Therefore, when I have done my part, I hope to go to the reward offered for the faithful. So, my answer is 'no.' I do not believe an immortality pill would change our faith, and I don't think I would want such a pill. I would rather go to heaven." To be honest, even I was surprised by

---

[9] Romans 6:8 (NAB).

my reasoning. This is not something I have thought much about, but I think it is accurate. The young boy seemed very satisfied with the answer I gave him.

Here is another example of the young offering enlightenment to immortality. One young man in his thirties was dying of cancer. I asked him if he was afraid. He said, "I'm not afraid of judgment. I trust in God's mercy and have asked forgiveness for my sins. I'm good with God, but I am still afraid. I do not seriously doubt heaven, but I do not know what it will be like. I feel like a child preparing for the first day of school. All the theories and images we are taught about heaven are pretty ambiguous: 'paradise,' 'kingdom,' 'angels,' 'free from suffering.' What will things look like without my body? What will I see as I look through the eyes of my new, resurrected body? Will I still be me without the physical wiring of this brain in this cancer-laden body?" An excellent point to contemplate. I have to admit, I have no clear answers. At the same time, there is a value in contemplating our final hope and Christ's promise of Heaven.

OTHER PRAYER TECHNIQUES

St. Ignatius of Loyola taught ***The Examen.***[10] In the morning, prayerfully visualize the agenda of the day. Can you anticipate any moments when you may be tempted? Can you foresee any situations or people you will encounter that typically stretch your need for spiritual fortitude? Will you see that person who annoys you? Or

---

[10] Ignatius of Loyola, *The Text of the Spiritual Exercises of Saint Ignatius*, 13.

that physically attractive person? Or that coworker that does not pull his own weight? Or that buddy that always pressures you into having one more drink? Ask for God's grace. Be prepared. At midday, look back at your morning. How did you do? Mentally walk through the morning, paying special attention to the presence of God and any internal movements, feelings, or prayers that occurred. Are there any people you need to apologize to? Make amends right away. Why wait? This is your chance to be holy! In the evening, examine the day again. This will help you to identify, prepare, and improve the way you apply virtue and a consistent Christian mentality throughout the day.

The Examen is not meant to cause you to become too self-critical. It is designed to help you take very seriously your efforts to improve. You are a work in progress, but you are making progress.

Another prayer technique to use throughout the day is to **Search for Potential Saints**. Honestly, I want to be a saint. I do not, necessarily, want fame or to feel righteous. I simply want to please the Lord. I want to let God into every aspect of my life and allow His grace to work through me. I want to fill the activity of my life with meaning. I am honored to be invited into the mission of the Church and the development of history. I want to inspire others to do the same. I want to reach the end of my life and hear the words, "Well done, my good and faithful servant."[11] Is that not what you want, too? Well, guess what? You want to be a saint, just like me. So now, look for those potential saints.

---

[11] Matthew 25:23 (NAB).

All people are called to be holy. There are some who diligently pursue the goal of holiness. They spend considerable energy aiming toward the life demonstrated by the Saints. Keep a vigilant eye out for those like-minded people who desire to be more than average. Actively look and inspire people to do the same. Motivate each other, like a group that exercises together or celebrates weight loss together. I cannot help but wonder if I have come across any true Saints. They must be out there. Even if the Church does not officially recognize me as one, what a great honor it would be to have helped a Saint succeed. Would it not have been joyful beyond words to know that you helped St. Augustine or St. Catherine to become a Saint? Even if I only did one little part, it would be an incomparable blessing! Right now, you are already part of the story of the life of some future Saint. Find him or her, and do your part!

Journaling is an excellent way to continue to develop your prayerful relationship with God. There are two benefits of journaling. First, it forces you to slow down your thoughts and put more consideration into what you really want to say to the Lord and what the Lord is saying to you. Our minds are so cluttered, and our thoughts race faster than we can process. It can be so hard to listen to the Lord when we are doing all the "talking" in our minds. Slow it down! Second, journaling helps us to organize our thoughts and progress toward spiritual maturity. We often have some very good and deep insights that seem to be forgotten as we move on to the next idea in our heads. Writing slows down this process and allows us to return to these insights and even develop these thoughts. The next time we pray, especially when doing a routine prayer like contemplating the Rosary, we often just rehash what we thought of last time. Writing it down gives us a chance to take that thought one step further. This will keep your prayers fresh and, hopefully, lead to new insights and commitments you otherwise would have missed.

Another method of prayer is to share some **Silence** with the Lord. I recommend silence while in Adoration of the Holy Sacrament. "Be still and know that I am the Lord."[12] There is no rule that says prayer has to be a bunch of words. Jesus preferred that we not imitate "...the pagans, who think that they will be heard because of their many words."[13] Just listen. Sometimes, God has something to share with you. Sometimes, God just wants to be quiet with you, too. When couples fall in love, there is a deepening of their intimacy when they can just be quiet together. Let the Lord guide the conversation or the lack thereof.

All day long the Tempter is talking in your ear, trying to get you to sin. How good it is to enjoy an hour in the Lord's presence, away from the distractions. We spend too much time with the Tempter's nagging. Now spend an hour with the calmness of the Lord. The Tempter may try to interrupt your hour. Be persistent. Though it takes about fifteen minutes to get used to adoring in silence before the Blessed Sacrament, the next forty-five minutes seem to fly by. You will be amazed at how refreshing it can be and how close you can feel to the Lord.

---

[12] Psalms 46:11 (NAB).

[13] Matthew 6:7 (NAB).

GOING TO MASS

Do not underappreciate the power of **Rituals** – the rituals of the Mass, Reconciliation, blessing ourselves with holy water, making the sign of the cross when passing a church, kissing a Miraculous Medal before putting it on, grace before meals, etc. When we greet people from foreign countries, there is typically a formal greeting. This act of bowing, shaking someone's hand, or saying a common greeting is a ritual that is meaningful across cultures. When children serve at Mass well, they enjoy the processions, the carrying of the cross, and the movements through the ceremony. The ritual involves them in the mystery. When I visited Sri Lanka, the parishioners in a Catholic community that was highly influenced by the Hindu culture met me at the door of the church. They bowed to me, blessed me with a candle, placed a lei over my head, and painted a red dot on my forehead. These were ritualistic signs that I was an honored guest. The children performed various dances, and, after my speech, they touched my feet as a sign of respect for a wise teacher.

All of these rituals go beyond the intellectual or even affective experience. It seemed to have touched a more basic part of our souls. Ritual seems to reach down to the universal human experience. It resonates with all cultures and ages. Imagine every day hearing someone say, "I love you." That makes a difference. Our ritualistic routines shape our reality and our outward perspective. Let the Rituals of the Catholic Church work on you.

It is an obligation to attend Sunday Mass (or the Vigil) each week.[14] Many people seem to think that they should go to Mass when it is convenient, or when they "need it," or only a few times a month or a year. It is still an obligation. The primary reason for the Mass is to adore God, receive the graces of the Sacred Scripture and the receive the Holy Eucharist. My mother used to say, "If I invited you to dinner and you said you were coming, then you didn't show up, I would be offended." Go to the Lord's Supper weekly, as is the obligation of Catholics. Do not offend the Lord by not taking seriously His invitation.

Sometimes we do not want to go to Mass, but we go anyway out of a sense of obligation. I believe this is **Worth Even More** to the Lord. If I go to a hospital to visit a sick friend, did I go because I like the sight of blood and the smells associated with the hospital and sick people? Do I go so that I can take over for the doctor and heal the sick person? Of course not. I went to see my friend. My friend knows that I endured the discomfort of being in a hospital because of my love and respect for him. Even if my friend is unconscious, there is a value to visiting him. Though it seems like I have done very little to help the condition of my friend's body, I may have helped his soul. Certainly, the visit has helped *my* soul. So it is when we go to Mass when we do not have the excitement or motivation to go. We went, not to be entertained or to do what we wanted to do, but out of love and respect for God and the other members of the com-

---

[14] *Catechism of the Catholic Church,* paragraphs 2180-2181.

munity. Even if we feel we did very little to contribute to the community or the world by our attendance, I assure you that the spiritual benefits to souls are just as real as visiting the sick in a hospital.

Another underappreciated reason for the Sunday Obligation is to foster the spirituality of **Community**. Though we are called to develop our personal relationships with Jesus, we are also members of His people. St. John made it clear that "…whoever does not love a brother whom he has seen cannot love God whom he has not seen."[15] Sometimes we wiggle around this inconvenience by avoiding people. Thus, the Church, in her wisdom, creates the opportunity for us to be in proximity with one another: Mass. Being together can inspire us and create opportunities to reconcile with each other. It can produce synergy to apply the Gospel to our daily lives and to our greater society.

For young adults, the community aspect of Mass is very difficult. Since it is so oriented toward families, and they have yet to begin their own families, they feel out of place. I understand this issue and continue to encourage them to support one another. If we "take a break" from Mass until we are married, we very well could lose the discipline of Mass attendance or even the faith itself. We need grace more than we know.

Some people say, "I do not get much out of Mass." This saddens me for two reasons. First, the parishes have not stepped up to the challenge of sufficiently feeding the flock in their care. This is their duty. And second, many people think of the Mass as something that should either entertain or stimulate them. The Mass requires some

---

[15] 1 John 4:20 (NAB).

effort both by the priest and from the congregation. Without proper feedback and suggestions, it is difficult for parish life to reach the needs of its parishioners. The lion's share of the responsibility is with the pastor. It is important to take seriously our role in listening, engaging, and evangelizing our people, regardless of whether they are disciplined in their attendance at Mass or not.

The young often hold the above complaint that the "don't get much out of Mass." There has been a disturbing trend not to require children and teens to attend Mass. In my experience at the parish, this mentality stems from two sources: First, parents resented when they were forced to go to Mass as kids, so they fear their children will feel the same way. Secondly, many think religion is about making us "good people." Since they believe their children are already "good people," there is no need for them to go to church. This misses the communal spirituality of praising God as a unified people and looking for opportunities to help and be helped by our fellow community members. In addition, the goal of a Catholic is far higher than to be a "good person." It is about becoming the disciples Christ deserves. Becoming disciples will require grace. To miss Mass is to miss out on the graces God wishes to impart on us.

It is true that we do not have to be in a church to pray. We can pray while sitting, driving, showering, etc. Yet, there is some value in occasionally getting down on one's knees. Jesus does not need me to kneel in a church to pray; I need to kneel in a church in order to remember to pray reverently. We call this virtue or spiritual gift, "**Fear of the Lord**." We are not "afraid," because we know God is a loving Father. Yet, we are aware God deserves our respect.

There are many people who claim that they are **Spiritual, but Not Religious**. This is different from those who consider themselves "not very good at practicing their faith." The second group at least recognizes that they should improve. The "Spiritual but Not Religious" group tends to feel righteous, free, and even a little arrogant toward those who congregate at a church. By distancing themselves from religion, they consider themselves "good" or "holy" without any criteria for determining their goodness or holiness. They do not hold themselves to any standards or obligations other than the ones they invent for themselves. These rules are usually a combination of the parts of religion they enjoy and appreciate without the challenges. In my experience, people who do not practice a religion soon stop having any recognizable routine of prayer. They claim they pray, but, in practice, they struggle to *actually* pray with any consistency. For those who are spiritual but in search of a religion, I applaud their efforts and encourage them to take seriously their commitment to finding a community where they feel comfortable and spiritually fed.

Some people are **Disillusioned** by the Church. Sadly, we, the members of the Church, especially the clergy, carry the blame for our sinfulness, scandals, hypocrisy, and mistakes. When people express their disillusionment about the Church, I cannot help but agree with them. The Church is called to be better than she is now. Perhaps those closest to the Church, who love her most, should be the most outraged. Before my ordination, many advised me to disassociate with the Church, especially with regard to the clergy sex scandals. I must admit, I was greatly tempted to forego my vocation. Prayerfully, I decided that it would not be good if all of the healthy people stepped away from the Church. We would simply be abandoning the Church to the hands of the wicked. Then, we would have thrown away a great gift. In addition, who would be left to stop the wicked if the good have all gone? I decided to step forward and become part of the reform. I want to help the Church become more of who she is supposed to be, who she is called to be. I want to become the disciple Christ deserves and the Church Christ intended.

Sometimes our disillusionment about the Church is exaggerated. We can be tempted to free ourselves from any moral obligation by dismissing the Church as being corrupt or unholy. Therefore, we claim to be holier than the Church. I recognize that members of the Church are sinners and are in need of ongoing conversion. However, I still believe the Holy Spirit is guiding the Church. God will not abandon us. Christ has promised.[16] Perhaps a better way to think of the Church, to borrow an image from Pope Francis, is as a **Field Hospital** for souls.[17] If I were to walk into a hospital, would I be shocked to see sick people? Of course not. Then why am I shocked to see sinners in the hospital for sick souls? If you are perfect, then the Catholic Church may not be what you are looking for; if you are a sinner hoping to become a saint, welcome to the Field Hospital for souls.

---

[16] Matthew 28:20b (NAB).

[17] Francis, "General Audience of 28 August 2019," General Audience of 28 August 2019 | Francis, August 28, 2019, https://www.vatican.va/content/francesco/en/audiences/2019/documents/papa-francesco_20190828_udienza-generale.html.

SACRIFICE

The supreme example of the Cross gives us the model of offering **Sacrifice** as a prayer. While no sacrifice can match the gift of the Cross, we are invited to unite our small sacrifices to the Crucified Lord. St. Paul gives a great example by considering all of the trials and difficulties he endured for the sake of the Church as being an oblation offered to God.[18] Do not be afraid to offer sacrifice. Transforming suffering into a sacrifice is the power of the Cross itself.

Our sacrifice should not be seen as a payment requiring something in return. Rather, it can be seen as an act of gratitude or an expression of the magnitude of our love for God. Imagine a boy offering a flower to a girl. Does it make a difference to the girl if the flower was plucked off the bush in front of her house as he approached the door, or if the boy risked life and limb to climb the highest mountain to find this rare flower for his love? In the same way, it matters to God that we offer the best we have, and not just lazily offer what is convenient. I saw pilgrims carrying heavy rocks up a mountain as a sacrifice to give thanks for favors received. Men crawl on their knees up the aisle at the Basilica of Our Lady of Guadalupe. It was a common practice for farmers to wake up at 3:00 AM to offer prayers when they had nothing else to offer. In their poverty, they were still able to offer a little bit of their sleep. Do not mock the poor man's faith. "Whoever mocks the poor reviles their Maker."[19] We, too, should appreciate the value of prayerful sacrifice.

---

[18] Romans 12:1 (NAB).

[19] Proverbs 17:5a (NAB).

EMOTIONS

One of the pitfalls of judging our prayer life is when we simply equate spirituality with emotions. Emotions are part of being human. God made us this way. Therefore, emotions are good, but that does not mean that we simply follow our feelings. The movies romanticize the idea that your heart knows what is best for you. Anyone with experience knows how foolish and fickle our desires can be. Yet, many people, including adults, continue to be slaves to their emotions. They do what they feel like doing, rather than what they are called to do. They sacrifice the long-term satisfaction for the short-term benefit.

Emotions can be very powerful. We sometimes mistake the intensity of emotions as being a greater truth or a sign from God. Emotions, by their nature, are temporary. If we simply comply with our momentary emotions, soon we will be living with the consequences of our actions without the emotional reward. Still, our emotions can be helpful indicators and tools for seeking the truth, though they are not truth in and of themselves.

Think of strong emotions as **Fire Alarms** sounding in a building. If the firefighters rush into the building only to find the alarm and turn it off, they have done nothing. They must find what made the alarm sound. They must find the fire. Emotions are the alarms that are triggered by some other reality. To discover the proper response to the emotion, we must first interpret its meaning and cause.

Try to imagine a person winning an award for some accomplishment. Feeling confident and optimistic, he turns to his wife and says, "Let's have a baby!" Why? Because you feel so good? Because it feels like the right time? There are other factors to be considered, prayers to be prayed, and a wife to be consulted. Maybe it is time for a baby, but emotions are not the proper measurement of that.

Another example might be if someone is applying for a job that has great potential and economic benefits. Imagine if the applicant turns down the job simply because it requires some basic mathematics which she can handle perfectly well. She describes her feelings as a "gut feeling that this is not the right fit for her." As we explore the feelings, we might discover that a fourth-grade teacher had ridiculed her for her math skills. The point is that emotions are not the highest priority of our lives. They are merely indicators of something deeper. We do not want to dismiss emotions, nor do we want to give them more authority than they deserve.

Sometimes we think that prayer is good when it makes us feel good. A good comparison would be with a married couple. Is it a good marriage when they feel good? There are many factors that might affect our emotions. It might be a perfectly good marriage, though the emotions do not correspond. In the marriage vows, the couple commit themselves to fidelity "in good times and in bad." This is a recognition that their feelings and their situation in life will have their ups and downs. Nonetheless, they promise to be faithful. In the same manner, our prayer life will have moments when we feel excited, moments when we feel bored, moments when we feel dry, moments when we feel hungry for more. The Psalms, which have been a constant source of prayer for millennia, cover the whole range of emotions, teaching us to give to God all that we are experiencing, the good times and the bad. Just because our feelings are constantly fluctuating does not necessarily mean that our prayer life is bad. It is best to remain consistent with your prayer routine throughout the ups and downs. It is a form of fidelity to the Lord. A spiritual director can help a person explore the real meaning of the emotion and discover if it is correlated to the quality of prayer life.

Emotions should not be discounted. Emotions are real and should be recognized, though they are not always indicative of the full truth. Especially with regard to emotions evoked from a communication perceived to be from God, the emotion may be an instrument that the Lord uses to guide us toward His Divine Plan.

LISTENING

Be Mindful of the Listener. Be careful, not only of what we say, but also of the way the message is heard and the way the listener reacts to the message. Sometimes we hide behind false righteousness, distancing ourselves from any responsibility for the way people feel after hearing our message. We disguise our insensitivity by claiming we are "just telling the truth." I believe that Truth is objective, but the communication of that truth is subjective. The truth does not change, but the way that we communicate that truth evokes an emotional response from the listener. Think about the goal of the conversation before speaking. When you speak, use expressions, intonations, examples, and all other forms of communication to elicit the response that best serves the person to whom you are speaking. As St. Paul tells us, "No foul language should come out of your mouths, but only such as is good for needed edification, that it may impart grace to those who hear."[20] If the goal is to challenge a person toward conversion, sugar-coating the truth of a criticism is inappropriate. If we want to lead a person out of despair toward hope, reminding them of all their mistakes is not appropriate.

Some people object to the idea of choosing words carefully while keeping in mind the emotion one wants to evoke in another person. Somehow they think this is inauthentic. I turn to Jesus for the example. When Jesus spoke to some people, His words seemed gentle and reassuring. For example, when Jesus spoke to the Samaritan Woman at the Well,[21] He was gentle in guiding her toward holiness. With other people, Jesus seems to speak harshly, for example, when He calls the Pharisees, "You brood of vipers!"[22] as He challenges their wrong way of thinking. On some occasions, Jesus seems unnecessarily harsh, such as when He says to the Canaanite woman who begged Him to cure her daughter, "It is not right to take the food of the children and throw it to the dogs."[23] Perhaps one way of understanding the inconsistency in Jesus' style of speaking is to realize that Jesus reads the hearts of the people. He knows exactly how each person will react to His message, and He chooses His words carefully to produce a specific response.

For most of us, we are guessing as to how a person will respond to our words. We can develop this skill by getting to know the listener, but we can never know a person's heart perfectly like God does. If you find that you were mistaken in your anticipation of the

---

[20] Ephesians 4:29 (NAB).

[21] John 4:4-42 (NAB).

[22] Matthew 12:34 (NAB).

[23] Matthew 15:26 (NAB).

response of the other, apologize. The phrase, "I am sorry," is underappreciated.

When we notice what we perceive to be a communication from God, we should take into consideration that God already knows the emotions that the divine message will evoke in us. God intentionally chose the words or promptings of the message, what to say and what not to say, with the goal of causing a response in us. St. Ignatius of Loyola advised those he spiritually directed to pay attention to the **Internal Movements**, or the emotions that we are feeling, when examining our spiritual lives.[24] Technically, "Internal Movements" feel the same as an emotion but may have its origins from the Holy Spirit, rather than from psychological processes. Taking a deeper look into the root causes of emotions can be helpful in understanding the desired plan of action that God is asking of us. Perhaps God wants us to stay the course of action we have begun and senses our intention to change paths. God would then send a message of encouragement. If God wants us to change our course of action, he may send doubt or chastise us. Perhaps God wants to initiate a new path. God will send a message of enlightenment. In addition, God knows when too much communication might take us off the right path. In these moments, God will be silent. With some reflection, we can trust that the Lord is guiding us in a way that is accessible and understandable because He already knows our hearts and the response we will have to His promptings.

---

[24] Ignatius of Loyola, *The Text of the Spiritual Exercises of Saint Ignatius*, 106-114.

CHASING THE FEELING

Often people chase good feelings. We call this **Emotionalism.** They are constantly looking for the next prayer technique, the next retreat, the next book, the next spiritual trend, the next church, the next bandwagon. If a person is changing too frequently, he may be falling in love with the emotions rather than falling in love with the Lord. Being with the Lord can be exhilarating and powerful. Especially at a moment of conversion, a personal encounter with the Lord, or a miraculous event, it is extremely joyful and motivating. These emotions are gifts from the Lord meant to verify His love for you and the source of your heart's true desire. The danger is that we all too often fall in love with the gift, rather than the Gift-Giver; the ring, instead of the Groom. We must stay focused on the Lord, or we can become like a dog chasing its tail, thinking joy is something we need to catch.

St. Mother Teresa of Calcutta wrote in her diary that she had a moment of great clarity and enthusiasm when she heard the Lord call her to begin the Missionaries of Charity.[25] The memory of that calling sustained her as she worked diligently and patiently through the frustrations of getting the community off the ground. Then, the consolation from the Lord stopped. She felt nothing. There was no joy, enthusiasm, or motivation. It was as if someone had turned off the faucet. Because she did not receive any message from God to change her course of action, she continued with her mission to the

---

[25] Mother Teresa, *Mother Teresa: Come Be My Light: The Private Writings of the "Saint of Calcutta,"* ed. Brian Kolodiejchuk (New York: Doubleday, 2007), 39-53 and 149-207.

poor and dying. She admitted that she struggled to keep going, and she begged God to give her some of those sweet emotions she once had. Finally, God did return the consolation, but only for one day. Then she was back in the spiritual desert for the rest of her life. Although it seems unfair, we must trust that God now showers Mother Teresa with joy beyond our imagination. Yet, her example shows us to continue the works of charity simply because it is God's holy Will that we do. Sometimes, we do good things seeking the reward of applause, or feeling like a good person, or consolation from our Lord. Even when she received no worldly or emotional reward, Mother Teresa continued to be faithful to God. She loved the Gift-Giver more than the gift of sweet emotions.

MANAGING OUR EMOTIONS

Negative emotions can be powerful. Fear is a typical obstacle that prevents people from following through with what they perceive to be God's Will. What will people think? What if I am not good at that? What if I fail? What if I start, only to find that I cannot finish? Fear, just like the other emotions, is merely a sounding alarm. Treat it as you would any emotion. Find the root cause so that you can respond appropriately. However, do not be ruled by fear. Fear can help us avoid injury or understand risks. A person with no fear is a liability. Eventually, he or she will prove to be imprudent. Fear is part of calculating risks. Yet, it is only an emotion. If we are to follow the Lord, we must conquer our fear, which is to say that it becomes a tool for holiness rather than a slave master. The lives of the Saints and the life of Jesus give us examples of how to acknowledge our fears, while not being ruled by them. It is through fear that we learn courage.

Some of our emotions can be so powerful that they may be dangerous to our souls. In particular, sexual attractions, being enamored, resentments, prejudices, self-hatred, aloofness, anger, bitterness, insecurity, egotism, and more. Some individuals may find it necessary to work with both a professional counselor and a spiritual director to achieve freedom from enslavement to these emotions.

Deliverance Ministry has had wonderful success in this area of spiritual freedom. The book *Unbound*[26], by Neal Lozano, has been helpful in my experience with deliverance ministry. It has a gentle way of looking at these negative emotions more like a cancerous tumor to be removed, rather than as a judgment on the holiness or goodness of a person. Most of the time, people have not chosen these negative feelings. Therefore, they do not know how to get rid of them. Deliverance Ministry asks for the Divine Physician to remove the "cancer" that is making us spiritually sick. I do see a parallel with the reliance on God's grace to deliver us from sins that enslave us and the first step of Alcoholics Anonymous: "We have become powerless."[27]

If following the Lord was easy, we priests would be out of a job. Take a good look at the Cross. There is nothing easy about following the Lord. If your spiritual life is too easy, you might be doing it wrong. When the consolation comes our way, filling us with joy and

---

[26] Neal Lozano, *Unbound* (United States of America: Chosen Books, 2010).

[27] "The Twelve Steps," Alcoholics Anonymous, 2024, https://www.aa.org/the-twelve-steps.

enthusiasm, give thanks to the Lord. When it goes away, stay faithful. Ask the Lord to give you the strength to endure the difficulties that are sure to be part of our lives. Being Christian is not about having fuzzy feelings and carefree lives. It is about facing the same challenges as all other people, but facing them with the most powerful tool in our armory: Grace. Grace[28] is God's life gifted to us in the Holy Spirit, in the Sacraments, in the Church, in our prayers, in the prayers of others, and in what I call Reciprocal Grace.

Reciprocal Grace is the blessings that come back to us for doing God's Holy Will. Sometimes we sense that Reciprocal Grace, and sometimes we do not. Yet, every time we perform the Spiritual and Corporal Works of Mercy, every time we are charitable in speech, attitude, volunteering, or donating, there is a benefit to our own souls. We learn to love more or "die to self" more. We feel excited about helping someone, or satisfied having behaved in a manner that pleases the Lord. Jesus tells us that it is better not to receive the reward in this life.[29] In other words, we forego the immediate, worldly rewards for the more precious reward that awaits us in heaven. At the same time, the confidence we have in presenting these works of mercy before the Judgement Seat of God gives us comfort and hope. "When you fast, do not look gloomy like the hypocrites. They neglect their appearance, so that they may appear to others to be fasting. Amen, I say to you, they have received their reward. But when you fast, anoint your head and wash your face, so that you may not appear to others to be fasting, except to your Father

---

[28] *Catechism of the Catholic Church,* glossary, "Grace."

[29] Matthew 6:1-4 (NAB).

who is hidden. And our Father, who sees what is hidden, will repay you."[30]

Because of Reciprocal Grace, I think it is important to allow others to help us. When others have a chance to be charitable to us, we often feel that we are somehow less than them, or that we are taking the help that someone else deserves more. Let them love you! They need the Reciprocal Grace just as much as you do. Be humble. You do not have to do it all or be the most generous of people. Being poor in spirit is allowing others to help. The kids in El Salvador would run up to my car to help me bring in the things I needed for Mass. Everything was contained in one backpack, but I would open it up so that each child had something to carry. It was meaningful to them that they could participate in the Mass. Let people participate in God's activity. Do not monopolize all the charitable work. Invite people to help. Invite even the poor, even those we serve, to sweep up, straighten out the clothing donations, wash the dishes, or just visit with you. Everyone could use a little more grace.

There was a story of a priest sitting on a park bench feeding the pigeons. A man in a suit and tie walked up and handed the priest a $100 bill. He said, "Father, help the poor with this donation." The priest looked up and said, "You help the poor. Come on. I'll take you over and introduce you to the guys in the soup kitchen." Too often we distance ourselves from the good work of the Church. We have made contributions and paid our taxes to many social benefits, yet we feel like we are missing something. What we are missing is the Reciprocal Grace. Charitable giving is better than being forced into

---

[30] Matthew 6:16-18 (NAB).

giving, such as with taxes. Relationship building is even better than charitable contributions. Clearly, charitable giving allows others to work with the funds to provide for those in need on our behalf. However, we would be remised if we never met or even thought about the recipients of such charity. That ambiguous feeling that something is missing might just be a divine invitation to roll up our sleeves and get to work for the Kingdom. Even after the warm, fuzzy feelings dissipate, stay faithful; keep working. It is now that we are truly preparing "treasure in heaven" rather than on earth.[31] When we learn to love people beyond merely feeling good about ourselves, the graces seem all the more powerful.

[31] Matthew 6:19-21 (NAB).

Chapter 2

Tuning in to God's Frequency

We believe that life and history are not completely random, but that there is a purpose and goal in the mind of God. God has a Divine Plan that is unfolding in time. This is sometimes called **Divine Providence**. Out of all of God's creatures, we seem to be the only ones capable of perceiving this plan at all, although our understanding of it is still quite limited. In addition, we are active participants in this plan. We are not merely spectators or pawns to be moved about on the board. "I no longer call you slaves, because a slave does not know what his master is doing. I have called you friends, because I have told you everything I have heard from my Father."[1] We seem to have some power over the way the plan unfolds. We do not believe that

[1] John 15:15 (NAB).

we are robotically or merely instinctually programmed according to our role in the Divine Plan. We believe that we have **Free Will**. We can choose either to cooperate with or to resist the invitation of the Lord.

Looking up at the motion of the planets in the solar system, the orderly laws of physics, the balance of an ecosystem, does it not all indicate that there is a plan in motion? We simply extend the idea that the God Who creates order in nature has a rhyme and reason for doing so. In addition, we are part of this great, unfolding plan that is being realized as we speak.

I can get so disappointed in myself and others for our misuse of Free Will. Sometimes I wonder if it would be better if we had no choice but to do the good and the holy. Of course, this shows my limited view and distrust of the Lord. God did not make a mistake when He gave us Free Will. In ways that I may never understand on this side of Paradise, it is best that humanity does have Free Will. I know this because God is perfect, and He decided to give us freedom of choice. Therefore, it must be perfect that we have Free Will, though I cannot understand how.

Some people argue that humanity seems to mess up the beauty of the created universe. Though there are good reasons to preserve the natural world, I think it is strange for humanity to attempt to have no impact on the world. Those who take this worldview want to preserve nature, untouched by humanity, as if the things of nature were ends in themselves. From this perspective, humans are merely a distraction or distortion of the natural world. This is not the Judeo-Christian understanding of the supreme place humanity holds in Creation. God made us uniquely able to exercise free will and reason in such a way that we are capable, and even commanded, to "...subdue the Earth."[2] We must recognize that the natural world is a gift, not just for us and for this generation, but for all generations. Therefore, we are called to be responsible stewards of the Earth. At the same time, we are not merely one more type of creature in the midst of the universe. We are not a nuisance or a weed to be minimized. We do not exist for the sake of the things of nature; the things of nature have been given to us. God has chosen us to be an end in and of ourselves, different from the other creatures which are means to an end. Soil might exist for plants, and plants for animals, and animals for food and clothing, but it always leads back to us. We exist for our own sake. God made us because He loves us.[3] This is not personal opinion or wishful thinking. This is revealed Truth.

Love requires a level of freedom to choose to respond in kind or to decline to return the love you received. You cannot force someone to love you. A teddy bear cannot love you. A dog may have affection for you, but it is not truly love since the dog does not have Free Will like humans do. To be honest, my dog probably has affection for whoever is holding bacon. The ability to genuinely love seems to be reserved for humans. In addition, God reveals something truly amazing: God loves us! Each of us and all of us. God loves so perfectly that all other loves are merely a reflection of the Divine Love. And we are invited to use our Free Will to respond to God's love with our own love.

---

[2] Genesis 1:28 (NAB).

[3] *Catechism of the Catholic Church,* paragraphs 342-343, 356-358.

What boggles my mind is that God loves an imperfect creature like me. I can appreciate that God is worthy of love because of His greatness, goodness, and holiness. Yet, I am infinitely less than Him in all ways. This humble recognition of the distance between the Creator and me, the creature, is, itself, a revelation of how awesome God really is. God loves us unconditionally.[4]

Most of us tend to be fickle in whom we chose to love. It usually has something to do with how the person helps us or makes us feel. Even spouses struggle to love each other more perfectly. The closest we can get to God's love here on Earth might be the love of a mother for her children. Once, when my siblings and I were children, my mother was taking a nap. She woke up to find us standing over her with a pair of scissors. We were playing barber shop. The only reason she did not throw us out of the second-floor window after we cut her hair is **Unconditional Love**.

When I am preparing couples for marriage, I usually ask them why they want to get married. They, of course, say that they love each other. (Interestingly, the people in El Salvador always responded that they wanted God's blessing). I then follow up by asking what they love about each other. They feel awkward as they list a whole bunch of good qualities. But the longer they talk, the more those tired answers seem unable to properly describe the reason they love each other. The more mature the individuals are, the more they realize that, even if those qualities change or fade, they will still love

---

[4] Benedict XVI, "Deus Caritas Est," December 25, 2005, https://www.vatican.va/content/benedict-xvi/en/encyclicals/documents/hf_ben-xvi_enc_20051225_deus-caritas-est.html, paragraph 1.

each other. They have a hard time naming why they love each other. They are stretching toward Unconditional Love.

God does not love me because I am cute, smart, strong, successful, kind, generous, holy, funny, or any of the other attributes that we typically think of as being reasons for falling in love. Certainly, we are far less beautiful, intelligent, and good than God. In the entire history of humanity, God surely has known people that far surpassed all our good qualities. In fact, we have so many flaws that we might consider ourselves unworthy of being loved. The more aware we are of how awesome God is, the more aware we are of how insignificant our positive attributes actually are compared to God. It is like claiming I am pretty good at golf while standing next to Tiger Woods. Now, I just look pathetic. Yet, that is precisely how magnificent and beyond all understanding the love of God is! The fact that God loves an imperfect person like me does not mean that God is a fool, mistaken, or blind. It means that the love of God is greater than my imperfection. God is even greater than I had imagined!

This is one of the great spiritual truths of the Faith: "**God is Greater Than I Can Imagine**." By definition, God is beyond my understanding. St. Augustine told a story about a little girl at the beach filling a hole in the sand with water from the surf.[5] St. Augustine asked her what she was doing. She explained she was going to put the ocean in the hole. St. Augustine explained how impossible that would be, since the hole was small and the sea was vast. The girl responded, "Yet, you really think your little mind could ever grasp the

---

[5] Jacobus de Voragine, *The Golden Legend*, trans. William Caxton, ed. George V. O'Neill (London: Cambridge University Press, 1914), 105-106.

immensity of the Divine?" Necessarily, we all fall short of understanding the true nature of God. After writing his tome the *Summa Theologica,* it is said that the dying St. Thomas Aquinas called it "all straw."[6] As he encountered the Divine with his last breath, he came to realize that all the theology of the greatest minds pales in comparison with the reality of God.

While we are aware that God is greater than we can imagine, we often do not reflect on the consequences of such a belief. It means that the concept you have in your mind about God is wrong, or at least not perfectly accurate. God is not Who you think He is! Each time we come to a new realization of the magnitude of God, we should be awestruck! Sometimes it fills us with wonder and excitement. Sometimes it fills us with fear and uncertainty.

It is not uncommon for those who are seeking spiritual direction either to have weak foundations in their understanding of God or to have already become disturbed that God is not fulfilling their expectations. When confronting an atheist, I think a good way to enter into a meaningful dialogue is to say, "Tell me about the god you don't believe in, because I probably don't believe in him either." I am assuming that the preposterous ideas of God that the atheist cannot accept are not at all the God I have come to know. So many times we think of God as a genie or a fairytale. We reduce God to a concept or an overly simplistic, even child-like, model. The Scribes and Pharisees, who were the most equipped to recognize Jesus as the Messiah,

---

[6] Alban Butler, *Butler's Lives of the Saints: Complete Edition*, Vol. 1, eds. Herbert Thurston and Donald Attwater (Westminster, MD: Christian Classics, Inc., 1956), 511.

also were confused and even angry that He did not match their expectations.

When we are very young, we think our parents are capable of anything. Even when we resist their efforts to properly form and protect us, we trust that they are probably right and the problem is us. At some time in our development, we come to realize that our parents are not superhuman. They are flawed, insecure people like the rest of us. Their decisions are really educated guesses. They are often inconsistent or hypocritical. They make lots of mistakes and are not perfect models. This can be quite unsettling and world-shaking for us. Hopefully, we make it through to the other side by recognizing that, precisely because of their humanness, we should be amazed with all that our parents were able to accomplish, overcome, sacrifice, and risk for our sake. It would have been easy for Superman. It was nothing short of heroic for our parents.

When God operates differently than we had anticipated, we become aware that God is not exactly who we thought He was. We often feel those same old traumas like we did when we realized our parents were not who we thought they were. With our parents, we could at least give up the notion that they are perfect. With God, He is always perfect; it is our concept of God that we have to abandon. It can shake the foundations of our faith when we see injustices in the world, when our prayers do not seem to be answered, when we realize that the Holy Bible is not all supposed to be interpreted literally, when we are called to love the worst of people, or when we recognize that God called sinners to run His Church. Yet, this is part of growing in a genuine relationship with God. God is not a topic we read about in a book. God is a real Person (technically three Persons in One God). Just like we cannot come to know a human person by reading about him or her on Facebook or through a résumé, if we are ever going to know Christ, we must encounter Christ in a personal and significant way. We must dialogue with God. Not only must we share with God all of our feelings, hopes, fears, and desires, but we must also let God do the same for us. We must learn how to listen to what God is telling us about Himself. God is revealing His Sacred Heart.

Through spiritual direction, we hope to guide people to encounter the Risen Lord, who is communicating and active in our lives. In the process, we come to know Christ personally and profoundly. The more we know Christ, the more we know Truth. Without Truth, we are merely wandering in the dark, groping for some sign of hope and guidance. Allowing Christ to reveal Himself to us will also reveal who we are in His eyes, the meaning of our lives and of history, and the way that we are to actively follow Christ as His disciples. The process is ongoing. To fully understand the Truth, we would need to be eternal, like God. We can only hope that God will reveal enough to us that we can serve Him sufficiently to please Him in this life.

As I have come to know God more intimately, He has revealed to me the **Sacred Heart of Jesus**. It is very heavy. While it is true that God does not change,[7] this does not mean that God is unaffected by our decisions and our suffering. Jesus, who is divine, feels the insults, the blasphemies, the pain, the sorrow, the shame, the rejections, the

---

[7] *Catechism of the Catholic Church*, paragraph 2086.

dying, the anguish, and everything else we are experiencing. It is revealed in the Passion of our Lord.[8] It is echoed in the reflections of the Saints. I feel it in my heart. So often, I want Christ to know what I am experiencing. I feel alone in my experience. Jesus feels the same way. Often, Jesus desires to share His perspective and heavy Heart with us. As we try to look at the world the way Christ does, we feel the gravity of the cost of Free Will. I cry for the sinners and their victims. I cry for the ignorant and the arrogant. I cry for those who are unaware that they are not alone. This is what my Lord feels. Yet, just as I find some consolation in unburdening my heavy heart with a trusted friend who really cares, I have to believe that, in my own small way, I comfort the Sacred Heart of Jesus with my desire to know and carry His burden.

To help others experience the weight of the Sacred Heart of Jesus and bring comfort to our Lord, I use a mental exercise of **The Agony in the Garden**. I invite the participant to close his eyes and imagine going into the Garden of Gethsemane.[9] It is the night before Jesus is to suffer His Passion. The Apostles have fallen asleep. Jesus is praying by Himself. You have the honor of listening to His pleading to the Father that this cup should pass from His lips. He fears pain and death. He feels alone and misunderstood. As He accepts the Will of the Father, the Sacred Scriptures say that the Father sends angels to tend to Christ's needs and bring Him comfort. That is your cue. Go to Him. Kneel with Him. Pray with Him. Tell Him you understand. Tell Him you are grateful for His sacrifice. Ask for forgiveness for

---

[8] Matthew 27:32-50 (NAB).

[9] Matthew 26:36-46 (NAB).

adding to the sins for which He would pay the price. Let Him know that, thousands of years from now, there will be a faithful person reflecting on this moment. Let the angels take your prayer through time and space back to Christ in that original garden. Let them deliver your prayer in a way that is more polished than our human words could ever mutter. Give this comfort to your Lord.

The intimacy with the Lord works both ways. Not only do we come to know Christ more personally and deeply, but we are invited to reveal ourselves to Him, as well. It may seem strange to think that we have to reveal anything to God. Nothing is hidden from His eyes. Yet, like Adam and Eve in the Garden of Eden,[10] we often hide from our Lord. It is foolishness, of course, but our God is so respectful of us that He will not enter where we have not welcomed Him. If you want Jesus to dwell in your heart, you cannot hold back from Him. You must be fully honest and transparent.

While there are many secrets of the heavens and the created universe, God has revealed to us exactly what we need to know in order to be saved. The Catholic Church does not believe, as some religions claim, that there are important spiritual secrets that are held by only a few.[11] All that needs to be known for our salvation has been revealed in the Person of Christ.

On the other side, we have no secrets that we can hide from God. Jesus often read the hearts of the crowds that heard His teachings and witnessed His miracles. Yet, we continue to hold onto our secrets? Why?

---

[10] Genesis 3:8 (NAB).

[11] *The Catholic Encyclopedia*, s.v. "Gnosticism."

Perhaps one of the reasons we hold on to the secrets of our hearts is that we have not quite finished processing our thoughts. The Virgin Mary is said to have "…held all these things in the secret of her heart."[12] Sometimes our secrets are a way to protect ourselves from others. Sometimes we guard other people's secrets for the same reason. We recognize that there are thoughts in our hearts that motivate our actions. We keep them secret so that others cannot use these motivations to manipulate us. We keep secrets so that people do not dismiss our opinions or contributions by rash judgment. Sometimes we hold on to our secrets because we simply do not want to admit that we are flawed and in need of help. We bury these secrets deep in our hearts and try not to think about them, pretending they are insignificant, while still using them to judge ourselves.

In general, we should be cautious about secrets. While it is true that we do not tell everyone everything we are thinking, we should be honest with ourselves and with our Lord. Honesty can be scary, but it is only scary before we reveal our secrets. Once we bring them into the light, they no longer hold power over us. We can then deal with them appropriately. In our prayer life, this kind of honesty requires our utmost confidence that God's love is unconditional, that we are lovable, and that God can heal us of whatever is bothering us. After all, God already knows your secrets and has already accepted you as His beloved.

The act of revealing an inner secret, especially one that reaches the core of your identity and the way you see yourself, takes a great deal of courage and trust in the one to whom you are revealing the

---

[12] Luke 2:51b (NAB).

secrets of your heart. A spiritual director can be an appropriate person for such revelation. This is why confidentiality and trust must be established. Leaving secrets in the dark simply delays the healing process and prevents the honesty required for a healthy prayer life. We must be willing to let Christ into every corner of our hearts. Nothing is held back.

When we intentionally keep secrets from our spiritual director, it often indicates that we do not want to change. We have become so accustomed to living with the darkness that the light of Truth will sting our eyes. We know we should not keep these things hidden, but we are comfortable with living with two versions of ourselves: the True self that is partially hidden and the self that we present to others. This is called "The Mask."

It sounds simple enough to be honest with the Lord. In practice, though, we have developed the bad habit of masking our real selves. We must apply the spiritual practice of **Unveiling the Mask**. To most people, we present ourselves as who we want them to see. We clean ourselves up, put on a specific style of clothing, prepare our hair in just the right way, and use vocabulary and expressions that give a calculated impression. While some of our unconscious or unscripted behavior may reveal more than we intended, for the most part we are successful in hiding behind the daily mask.

Before we start unveiling the mask, permit me to explain three functions of the mask which can be beneficial and practical. First, if your surgeon is having a bad day, you really do not want him throwing things and swearing before he grabs the scalpel. He is required to be professional. We, too, must be professional. If we find ourselves disgusted, attracted, annoyed, humored, bored, or other such emotions, there is no reason why we have to let everyone know about it. The world does not revolve around us and our feelings. Most people do not want to know. In many cases, it would be a distraction from what is most important. Be professional.

Another appropriate use of the mask is what Alcoholics Anonymous refers to as, *Fake It Until You Make It.* It means that we are aware that we are unrefined people. We are still developing toward the people we hope to become. We may occasionally go through the motions or say or do things that do not correspond to what we are really feeling inside. We train our hearts by acting like the people we want to be. We may pretend to be patient until it becomes effortless. We may give the impression that we are not easily offended until we are sufficiently confident. We may indicate that we have forgiven someone while continuing to complete the healing process in private.

The final beneficial use of the mask is to avoid entering into an inappropriate level of intimacy. Sometimes we hide our true feelings of attraction, love, or even suspicion or anger as a way of protecting ourselves and others from slipping into an emotional attachment or resentment that is not appropriate. If you are married or clergy, you must be careful of your boundaries with others so as not to further romantic feelings. If you are asking someone who is highly influenced by you to make a decision, it would be disrespectful to first reveal your preferences. If people are acting imprudently or scandalously, it may be wise for you to keep them at a distance until they address their issues.

The problem with the mask is that you can begin to believe that the mask is what people love about you. It is an idealized version of the person you want to be, but not the real you. You want people to think you are confident when you are not. You want people to think you are tough when you are scared. You want people to think you are sensitive, kind, generous, compassionate, and caring, when you are really struggling with self-centeredness and self-hatred. Since most people only see the mask, they are not able to help the real person underneath develop. We live in fear that, if people saw our real selves, they would be disgusted. We believe that we are merely disappointments wrapped in likeable masks.

When couples go on a first date or an interview, they usually put their best foot forward. They want the other person to like them. They feel the need to protect themselves from judgment, rejection, and ridicule. Some people have such deep insecurities about their true selves that they intentionally keep their relationships superficial. This prevents anyone from seeing beyond the mask. This is especially true of those struggling with addictions to drugs, alcohol, pornography, gambling, eating disorders, or other socially embarrassing vices. Because they do not allow anyone to see their true selves, they feel alone and unsupported in their attempts to heal or improve.

God, of course, is very aware of our struggles and our true selves. It would not be shocking for the Lord to discover our vices. The problem is that we do not let the Lord work with us on our true selves. We delude ourselves into thinking that if we never address the issue, then it is not a big deal. We pretend that God has already glanced over it and ignored it. We prefer to think that God is satisfied with most of our lives and leaves these parts out of the conversation. We secretly worry that if God took a good look at our real selves, He would realize how unlovable we really are.

The Truth is that God already loves us, unconditionally. All of the nonsense we tell ourselves in order to avoid being intimate with the Lord is coming from Satan. I know that it is difficult and humbling to focus on our secret, intimate flaws, but that is the only way the Divine Physician can begin to heal us. We must take down the mask. In our brokenness, we must accept the love of Christ. We desire to become better disciples, better people. God desires the same thing. Do not try to work on this by yourself and then present to the Lord a finished product. It will become procrastination that leads to failure. After all, no one can hold you accountable for progressive change in your spiritual life if you are not honest about what lies beneath the mask.

The fourth and fifth steps of Alcoholics Anonymous are about making an inventory of the exact nature of our transgressions and then revealing this to another person.[13] In a more general sense, it is the practice of naming and accepting responsibility for our sins and sinful inclinations. Then, we can be held accountable by another person for working to break our bad habits and addictions. A spiritual director can be an excellent tool to help us reveal our true selves, without the masks, and begin to work on becoming the disciples Christ deserves. As the steps of Alcoholics Anonymous remind us, we are not able to accomplish this change on our own. We

---

13 "The Twelve Steps."

are going to need the grace of God. But there is hope. The real you is already loved. Now let's work together to polish up that soul.

Chapter 3

Is That You, God? Discernment

Saying that God is "great" does not do justice to the greatness of God. God is **Mystery** Itself. The term, "mystery," in Catholic spirituality, does not mean that I know nothing about God, but that I cannot know everything about God. God is knowable, but not fully knowable. The things of creation can be described, measured, quantified, and qualified. "The marble is blue, round, and hard. The elbow is pink, bent, and soft." Yet, God can only be described to a certain extent. God is good, all-powerful, loving, eternal, etc. Whereas the created world can be studied using the senses, instruments, and the scientific method, God cannot. No matter how high I jump or how powerful my telescope, I cannot steal a glimpse of God in the heavens. There are even arguments about whether or not the masculine pronoun, "He," is an accurate or acceptable term to use for God. Though we are unable to grasp its entirety, what we have come to know about God was given to us in two ways: By rational induction, and by revelation.

Thinking in reverse, because we know that God is the Creator of everything, we also know that all of creation is God's artwork.[1] Just like with human art, we can come to know something about the artist by the fingerprints, themes, colors, and medium of the art. We look to nature, including human nature, as clues to the Divine cause and purpose of it all. This is called rational induction.

Revelation has to do with information about God that would have been impossible for us to induce simply by observing nature, no matter how smart of a supercomputer we used. It is information God Himself had to supply to us. Many of the theological and spiritual ways that we describe God go beyond logic and reason. How is God three Persons in one God? How can Jesus be fully human and fully divine? How can God be perfectly just and love a guy like me? Though they are puzzling, we hold these Sacred Mysteries to be true.

One of the major functions and roles of the Catholic Church is to be the guardian of the **Deposit of Faith**. Though we are still in a great dialogue about how to express the mysteries of Faith accurately, we are held to a solemn promise not to change, add to, or take away from what has been revealed to us by God.[2] The Deposit of Faith is a collection of revelations handed down over the centuries

---

[1] Ephesians 2:10 (NAB).

[2] *Catechism of the Catholic Church*, paragraph 84.

by a continual community of believers. Much, though not all, of the revelation has been recorded in the Sacred Scriptures. We believe the prophets, authors of the books of the Bible, and the teaching authority of the Church have all been inspired by the Holy Spirit to express and interpret accurately our foundational beliefs. We also hold that Jesus Christ is the fullness of that revelation.[3] This means we do not believe there is anything essential to our salvation that has not been revealed. There are still many questions, but, apparently, those answers are not required for us to go to Heaven. Everything we need to know has been given to us. We are not expecting any new or secret revelation.[4]

This does not mean that God has finished communicating with humanity. Throughout the history of the Church, in particular with the reception of the Holy Spirit on Pentecost and in the witness of the many Saints in history, God has continued to "speak" with men and women. Most people who are committed to a life of prayer have some sense that God has communicated with them, either as nagging feelings, events that are more than coincidences, or even messages that seem to enter, not through the ears, but deep down, internally. When there seems to be some revelation to an individual, it is called a **Private Revelation.**[5] A legitimate Private Revelation will not add anything new to the Deposit of Faith. It will be in agreement with the Deposit of Faith and is meant for the individual person and his or her circle of influence. It is usually very exciting and beautiful. You readily share the message you have received, but with whom

---

[3] *Catechism of the Catholic Church,* paragraph 65.

[4] *Catechism of the Catholic Church,* paragraph 66.

[5] *Catechism of the Catholic Church,* paragraph 67.

can you share it? Are people going to think you are hearing voices? Spiritual direction is a safe place where we can take seriously the analysis of private revelation and prayer dialogue with the Lord.

We should be very interested to hear what the Lord has said, even if God communicated with someone else. If a person said he was walking down the hall in the Vatican and Pope Francis came up to him and said something, would you want to know what he said? How much more should we be interested when it was God who shared even a word with one of us? I absolutely believe that God communicates with us, and I am fascinated to know what He has said to others.

We still have to address an important question: Is this message really from God? Let's begin by focusing on language.

What is the language of God? In my prayer life, I often think of Jesus speaking to me in English (or Spanish). The problem is that, in the first century, English did not even exist as a language yet. Jesus historically spoke Hebrew (Aramaic), and probably knew Latin and Greek (Coine). So, when I claim to "hear" God communicating with me, what language does He speak?

Though I do not doubt that there is no language God could not speak, it is probably closer to the truth that God communicates in a way that is meta-lingual, or even in **Pre-Lingual Communication.** When I hold my baby niece and speak softly to her, she responds as if she understands me. Her eyes get bigger. Her feet kick. A little smile develops. And she even coos back to me. I know she does not understand the words, but she seems to grasp the meaning based on the tone of my voice, my expressions, and the attention she is getting. It might be that God speaks to us in the same way. After all, whereas I am significantly more sophisticated than my baby niece, God is infinitely more sophisticated than me. A single utterance from God would be immeasurably more meaningful than all the sentences I could ever say. Perhaps that is why we hold so dearly the theology that Jesus is the singular, unique, creative Word of God that existed before all time.

If God speaks to me on a deep level that resonates more with my humanity rather than with my learned vocabulary, why do I describe the message from the Divine as if it were in English? The reason is that I am translating what I interpret to be the message of God. This is why it is not uncommon to find significant difficulty in explaining to someone what a spiritual moment was like. We even have a pre-lingual expression for it: the A-HA moment.

God mysteriously communicates with us in various forms. It can be a word or phrase that pops into our minds seemingly out of nowhere. It can be a theme that seems to be repeating through conversations, studies, or other media. It can be a jarring feeling that we struggle to articulate. It can be a message someone else has received in prayer. It can be those events that, on the surface, appear to be coincidences, but help guide us to the path where we find affirmation that we are right where we should be. I call these various ways of Divine Communication "**Promptings By the Holy Spirit**." Once received, they must be interpreted as a meaningful message that can then lead us either to deeper Truth or the Divine Plan.

The problem with serving as the recipient of a message while simultaneously being the translator and interpreter is that it can be confusing. How do I know that I am not just fooling myself? Maybe it was just a thought in my mind that I attributed to God. It is a little bit like listening to someone talking on the phone to your doctor and your lawyer at the same time. He tries to relay the messages accurately but fails to tell you which person said which part. It can become very confusing if you associate a sentence with the wrong speaker. "He says you only have two weeks." "Really? I have two weeks to live?!" "No, the lawyer says you have two weeks to finish the case."

Inside of your mind, there are multiple "voices" that all sound exactly the same because you are the translator. In spiritual direction, I often use the discernment technique of **The Four Voices**. The first voice is the **Voice of God**. That is the one we are trying to verify. There are further techniques for assuring that this voice is authentically from God, but the Four Voices is a good first step.

The other voices are the Ego, the Projected Voice, and the Tempter. The **Ego** is the individual. It is you mentally "speaking" to yourself. In this model, the Ego is not bad. It is just your thoughts, desires, hopes, and worries. You are good. God wants you to be an active participant in His plan. Though we often speak in pious terms about "losing the self," I believe God wants you to be directly involved in the creation of tomorrow. God is communicating *with you* and not just doing the plan without you. God expects you to engage your intellect, gifts, creativity, and so forth. The only thing to remember is that *you* are not God.

To properly distinguish the voice of the Ego from the voice of God, we must be brutally honest with ourselves. How does the message in question affect me? Is it to my benefit? Does it release me from something I was dreading? I find that we sometimes fool ourselves to avoid difficulties or responsibilities. Other times, we are hopeful that God agrees with our hopes and dreams. In my experience, it is rare for God to communicate in such a powerful way simply to say, "You know your plan? That's just what I was thinking!" It is more typical of God to intervene when He wants to change our course of action. Messages from God are usually surprising and seems a bit "out of the blue." The key is to be honest about how the message matches your own thoughts, desires, hopes, and plans. That being said, there is nothing wrong with your own thoughts, desires, hopes, and plans. Just be careful not to claim that they came from God, giving them supreme authority, rather than from your Ego.

The next voice is the **Projected Voice**. This includes the voices of all the people who influence you. Some of them are your heroes, friends, and family members, especially your parents. Some of them are your anti-heroes, those who criticize you, or those you do not want to imitate in any way. Again, these voices are not bad; they are just not God. We need our role models to help us figure out who we are supposed to be and who we are struggling not to become. It is helpful to occasionally make an inventory of the people who have most influenced you. When you sense a communication might be from God, test to see if there is someone else in your memory who planted the seed. It is perfectly acceptable to recognize that people have influenced the direction you have chosen to follow in life. It might even be holy and according to the Divine Plan. At the same time, just because your mother always wanted you to become a priest does not mean that God is calling you to ordination.

My classmate, Fr. Damian, is a fantastic priest. One of his many talents is playing the guitar. The youth group loved it when he acted like a rock star. Then he would take the group through a deep, philosophical, and theological conversation about beauty, holiness, sacrifice, and more. I greatly admire Fr. Damian. But, I am not Fr. Damian. And that is O.K. When I am with Fr. Damian, I sometimes feel the desire to be on stage, inspire the youth with high energy and deep thinking, and have fun doing it, just like he does. Sometimes I mistakenly think that God is calling me to do something like this. Then I realize that I am just admiring my friend. It is not God speaking in my head; it is Fr. Damian or, more specifically, my projected voice of Fr. Damian. He has been a great inspiration to me, but I have to be careful not to mislabel from where this prompting to be like him originates.

That being said, God can communicate to us through other people. When He does so, it is usually a surprise. I did not want to become a missionary and live in El Salvador. It was not an option until I had been ordained for five years. After my fifth anniversary, I prayed, "Alright, God, I said I would discern the missions at this point of my life. I know You're not going to call me. I hate the tarantulas, and I'm scared of the violence. I'm already doing so much in Hispanic Ministry in Cleveland. I've told absolutely everyone I know that I don't want to be a missionary. But, if You want me to go, I will say yes. But You better make it really obvious. Otherwise, I'll just keep developing the good things I'm doing here." That same day, three different people, totally oblivious about my prayer and the five-year requirement, asked me if I was going to be a missionary. So I signed up for six years in El Salvador. I find that God can communicate with us in many ways. It is up to God how He chooses to do so.

Back to the Four Voices. There is one more voice to recognize. It is the **Voice of the Tempter**. The Tempter is real, but we need not be afraid. The Tempter often uses our fears and our pride to pull us away from God's plan. Those are not the only weapons he has available. The key is to be honest about your temptations. We are all painfully aware of our own temptations, but we rarely ever talk about them. Again, the spiritual direction session is a safe place to converse about such spiritual realities. We all have temptations, even Jesus.[6] The important question is: How do we respond to our temptations? Do we choose to indulge them and stay enslaved to them, or do we turn to God when we are feeling weak?

Some common temptations are greed, sloth, intoxication, sex and the need to be attractive, false elevation of status or how other people view you, playing the victim, jealousy, resentment, and lies or half-truths. If you identify a thought from the Tempter, you immediately shut him down! You do not converse with the Tempter. So many people desire to understand the root cause of their sinful inclinations, but they find themselves wrapped in a twisted web of deception. This is what you need to know about the Tempter: He is smarter than you. He is cunning and has no qualms about being inconsistent with his methods. He does not desire your love or attention, only to distract you from God. There is no point in exploring the nature of the Tempter. If you study all there is to know about the Tempter, that knowledge would not save you. Your only defense is Christ. He is enough. Compared to Christ, the Tempter is less than a mosquito swatted away. Just like Peter walking on water, if you

---

[6] Matthew 4:1 (NAB).

look away from Christ, you will begin to sink.[7] Cry out to your Lord, and He will save you. It is that simple. Cry out.

When I hear someone I am directing say things like, "I'm just afraid that…" I realize that the Tempter is pulling at his heart. We stop the dialogue and enter into prayer immediately. Fear is not always bad. It is just safer to bring it to the Lord. "Lord, sometimes I am afraid. There are many things I cannot foresee. I am deep in the shadow of the valley and can only see the next step. Yet, You are on top of the mountain viewing the whole path. Lead me, Lord. I trust in You."

While we do not dialogue with the Tempter, we are permitted to name our temptations. We own them as our weaknesses and as a gift we give to the Lord. It is good to have someone like a spiritual director with whom we can be so honest about how much we need Jesus.

FURTHER DISCERNMENT

There is one devious trick the Tempter has in his arsenal that is invisible to the tempted. Borrowing the term from St. Ignatius, it is called the "**Angel of Light**".[8] The Angel of Light appears to be good, but it is the Tempter in disguise. The tempted will never be able to see this Angel of Light, as if a person were looking directly into bright headlights. For those outside of the beam of light, however, it is clearly not God. Perhaps this is why Jesus sent the disciples out

[7] Matthew 14:30-31 (NAB).

[8] Ignatius of Loyola, *The Text of the Spiritual Exercises of Saint Ignatius*, 112.

two-by-two and why He said, "Where two or three are gathered together in my name, there am I in the midst of them."[9] It takes another person to recognize the deception. Alone, the tempted will not see it. The other person does not even have to be highly trained in spiritual matters. It only requires a person who takes seriously spiritual discernment.

An example of the Angel of Light is when a young woman is head-over-heels in love with the wrong man. She is absolutely convinced that it is God's calling for her to marry this man. Everyone else can see the problem. Perhaps he is already married. Perhaps he is abusive. Perhaps he has a problem with addiction. Perhaps he is a scam artist. No matter what people tell her, to the young woman, all those defects are invisible. Hopefully, she has a trusted spiritual director who can help her avoid a big mistake. Afterward, she may be surprised at how blind she was.

This is just one example. Others feel called to abandon their families, their careers, even their Church. Some feel called to get revenge or belittle someone in the name of justice. Some feel called to commit suicide to escape their pain or shame. In each of these cases, know that the person is not, necessarily, mentally insane. They may have simply been deceived by the cunning Tempter as the Angel of Light. Use prayer, patience, and firmness to wake them up. Rely more on God's Grace than on logic and reasoning.

Though it may seem difficult to recognize the Voice of God, trust that you know God well enough to do so. "**The Shepherd** knows His

---

[9] Matthew 18:20 (NAB).

sheep, and His sheep know Him."[10] A few years ago, a woman came into my church with her seven-year-old daughter. They were both crying. They explained that a woman, who called herself the "Prophetess," told my parishioner that her daughter's sickness would end in death because God was angry that she was Catholic. They were both panicked. I calmed them down and asked the little girl, while her mother listened, "Does that sound like Jesus? Does it sound like Jesus to punish a little girl for picking which Church she wants to be a part of in order to worship God? Does that sound like the Jesus you know to threaten a little girl with harm or death?" She shook her head, indicating that it did not sound right to her. Then I continued, "You see, you belong to Jesus. You are His sheep. The sheep of the Shepherd know His voice. You didn't recognize this voice, so you know it wasn't Him. When you were confused and afraid, where did you go? You came to the House of God. You looked for God's priest to help take away your fear and tell you the truth. I am very proud of you. I assure you, God is not angry. God does not punish little girls with death. Jesus would not threaten a person just because they belong to this Church or that. I think you can see it clearly now. That woman lied to you. She claimed she is a prophetess. No, she is a liar. But you, good sheep of the Good Shepherd, are not fooled. You are going to be fine." They walked away, light as a feather, almost skipping down the street. Trust me, with a little discernment, you will recognize when it is authentically the Voice of the Good Shepherd and when it is a lie. Let me teach a few more discernment methods to aid in this important endeavor.

---

[10] John 10:3-4 (NAB).

TRUST BUT VERIFY

If we have discerned that a message does not seem to have originated from the Ego, the Projected Voice, or the Tempter, there is a good chance it is a genuine communication from the Lord. The next step in discernment is to "**Cross Verify**" the message with the Deposit of Faith.

Since we know that God is eternal, we know that God is the same yesterday, today, and forever. Therefore, if God reveals a message, it will be consistent with the Revelation that has been passed down over the generations. A good spiritual director should be able to identify, at least in general, whether this private revelation matches the official Revelation in the Deposit of Faith. Are there Scripture passages that verify (or contradict) the message? What about Vatican documents, official teachings, Fathers of the Church, theologies? Are there Saints that reiterate the same message?

The Vatican II document *Dei Verbum*[11] teaches a process for proper interpretation of the Sacred Scripture. It includes this concept of Cross-Referencing. Since the God of the Old Testament is the God of the New Testament and all of the books of the Bible were inspired by the one Holy Spirit, any interpretation must pass the test of verification with the other books. There should not be any contradictions. Any perceived contradictions will guide proper interpretation. I use the same method for discerning the authenticity of a private revelation. If there are inconsistencies, we do not follow the

[11] Paul VI, "Dei Verbum."

voice. If the private revelation is consistent with the teachings of the Church, we follow it.

Another method of verifying the authenticity of a perceived message from God is through reflection on what I call your "**Anchor Experience**." Your Anchor Experience is that key moment in your life when you are most confident that God intervened and communicated to you in some way. It might be a word, an idea, an event beyond coincidence, or a miracle. Though other people may have their doubts about whether your Anchor Experience was really from God, dismissing it as a merely natural or psychological event, for you, it was an important part of your story and a significant shift in your perspective on life and in your relationship with God. You are confident in its authenticity.

Any authentic Anchor Experience must be filled with meaning and layers of profound truth. After all, it is God communicating. Just like revisiting biblical passages many times, it is worth reflecting often on our Anchor Experiences. As we develop in life, those experiences will impact us differently. It is like listening to a recording of your heavenly Father's voice over and over again, discovering every nuance and deeper meaning.

Using the Anchor Experience, you can now direct your attention to the current message you are trying to discern. There should be some consistency between the old and the new message. There should be something familiar about the way the new message is presented and impacts you since this is not the first time the Lord has communicated with you. The God of your younger days is still the God of today. Though we change and develop and our situations vary, God is constant. Do you see any parallels in the two messages?

Do you recognize the way it was presented to you? Or are there any significant inconsistencies? Did God say one thing at this point and another back then? If you discover inconsistencies, it simply means that you should not act on the current perceived message until there is more clarity. Be patient. Take seriously the discernment process. Do not become overly excited to the point of being imprudent. If you do, you may run the wrong way or inadvertently follow the wrong voice.

UPON FURTHER REFLECTION

A more common method of verifying the authenticity of a Private Revelation is by **Looking to the Fruits**. St. Paul lists the Fruits of the Spirit in his letter to the Galatians: "…the Spirit produces love, joy, peace, patience, kindness, goodness, faithfulness, humility, and self-control."[12] In other words, if you are following the instructions of an authentic communication from God, it should result in the Fruits of the Spirit. If you do not experience the Fruits of the Spirit, you may have taken a wrong turn. This technique is a way of looking back on a decision to follow what you perceived as a Private Revelation. It is helpful to humbly analyze your past attempts to interpret the Divine Will.

No one discerns and interprets God's plan perfectly accurately every time. If we make a mistake, we simply back up and try again. We learn from our mistakes and try to identify where our interpretation or discernment went wrong. We then recognize the mistake

[12] Galatians 5:22 (NAB).

as being a weakness or a tendency we have toward obscuring the message. Perhaps we allowed one of the other voices to confuse us. Once we are aware of our tendency toward confusion, we will be more apt to pay attention to that flaw in the future. God, of course, is pleased that we are trying to follow Him. Though we may have gotten lost on the way, the Lord can still work with us, so long as we are not so prideful as to be perfectionists. God accepts our weaknesses, so we must accept them as well. If it were vitally important to God's plan for us to avoid a particular mistake, it would be up to God to be less ambiguous. Apparently, the message we received was enough to begin a series of events that pleases the Lord, even if we did not get it perfectly right.

The last method I use for discerning Private Revelations is **Find the Patterns**. Honestly, using this method has often led me down the wrong path, but I still think it has some value. Sometimes we imagine patterns that are not there. We look at clouds and see animals. We see a plant with eyes, only to realize it is a butterfly. We interpret someone's attitude as being a criticism of ourselves when he was actually going through a personal issue. At the same time, we are designed to recognize patterns. We can recognize a friend simply by the manner in which the silhouette is walking. When someone asks us to "wash the dishes," it is understood that we should wash the cups too. We run to someone's aide when we see an expression of pain on his face.

When it comes to spiritual direction, I help people notice patterns in their lives that indicate either a Divine Plan unfolding or a common tendency toward confusion. Looking at the communications I have received from God over the years, is He leading me somewhere? Is God preparing me for some task? Is God molding me in such a way that pleases Him? If I discover the pattern, perhaps I can anticipate the next step toward the goal God is setting. Often, I pray, "Lord, I think I know what You want me to do. I'm going to make decisions toward that goal. If I am wrong, please intervene and set me on the right track." I do not pretend I have information that has not been provided. I humbly make a judgment call and ask for continued guidance. Remember the prayer of Thomas Merton: "The fact that I think I am following your will does not mean that I am actually doing so. But I believe that the desire to please you does in fact please you."[13]

The second use of the method of Find the Patterns is to recognize the errors we consistently make. Many people lament that they confess the same sins every time they go to the Sacrament of Reconciliation. Yet, that makes perfect sense. Do you want new sins? These are the sins that stem from our personal temptations. Some temptations are more difficult to resist, depending on the person. For example, I do not struggle much with the temptation to steal. I do struggle with bending the truth to make myself look less culpable. When we Find the Patterns of how we get derailed from the Divine Plan, we are simply recognizing our blind spots. It is not so much that we are judging our worthiness or goodness, but that we are accepting the truth of our temptations. "These are my temptations. If I am not careful, my pride, lust, ambition, insensitivity, insecurities,

---

[13] Thomas Merton, *Thoughts in Solitude* (New York: Farrar, Straus & Cudahy, 1958), 83.

etc., will steer me off course. I will pay special attention to these motivations and pressures in my thought process and decision making, as well as in my discernment of God's Will for me."

For this reason, I am **Grateful for My Failures**. Sometimes my failures inadvertently serve the Lord's Plan. If everything had worked the way I had planned, I would be a married chemist instead of a priest. Yet, I am grateful that I am a priest. If I am sufficiently humble in my reflections, I can see in my failures a pattern of weakness. I have become more aware of myself and, therefore, more prepared to adjust my methodologies to counteract those mistaken tendencies. At the very least, my failures remind me that I am not in charge or as significant as I pretend I am. I still need a Savior. I have given the Lord one more chance to be patient and merciful to me, thus revealing His Love. I try not to focus on how bad I am or how good I am supposed to be. Instead, I focus on God's greatness. "Lord, You are infinitely more capable of doing everything You desire than I am. Yet, You invite me to participate in the formation of tomorrow. I thank You for the honor. Thank You for Your patience and Your mercy when I try to do it without You. The whole point is to work together, hand-in-hand with You, my Lord. I will do my best, though it is comically insufficient. Yet, You are so great, You will make up the difference where I fall short. You are so kind and loving to me. I truly love being Your beloved disciple."

To adjust our plan of life according to the Divine Plan and God's "veto power", we must be sufficiently detached from desiring any specific goal or outcome. I call this "**Holy Indifference.**" It is a concept from St. Ignatius of Loyola.[14] Holy Indifference does not mean that I do not care about the goal or outcome of a decision. Rather, it means that God's Plan is more important than my plan. I must be willing to accept the answer I receive in prayer. Like the expression, "Don't ask the question if you can't handle the answer," I have to be courageous and humble enough to be open to whatever God decides, even if it is not what I was hoping would be the decision. For example, I might desire to be assigned to an inner-city parish. I might desire it very strongly. However, if, in the process of discernment, it becomes apparent that God wants me to be in a rural parish, can I accept that answer? Even before I know the conclusion of the discernment, I must be open to the possibility that God has a different plan than I do. When I was discerning becoming a missionary, I had to consider the consequences of taking the decision out of my hands before I could make the commitment to being open to God's Will. "What if God wants me to go? Could I be free enough to say, 'Yes'?"

The alternative to Holy Indifference is to skew all messages, signs, and patterns to match my preconceived plan. I call this **Force Fit**. Like forcing a square peg into a round hole, I desperately try to force God's communication to agree with my desires. This is, of course, the opposite of discernment.

The truth is that we do not fully know what we want. As I mentioned in the Purifying Prayer technique, there are deeper desires in

---

[14] Kevin O'Brien, *The Ignatius Adventure: Experiencing the Spiritual Exercises of Saint Ignatius in Daily Life* (Chicago: Loyola Press, 2011), 63.

our hearts that, often, we, ourselves, do not recognize. We have to trust that God sees further and more profoundly than we do. Do we truly believe that God is good? That God loves us? That God's Plan is holy? Then **Let the Holy Spirit Drive**. Stop grabbing the wheel. We are allowed to have hopes, dreams, desires, and plans. We are not allowed to put any of them above God and His Plan. If we trust Jesus, we ought to trust the Holy Spirit that He sent to us. The Holy Spirit will always make a better decision than we could ever conceive.

One of the mistakes I sometimes make is to **Put Words into God's Mouth**. Sometimes I try to hear what I want to hear. When I was called to be a missionary, though I did not want to go, I trusted in the Lord. I figured, "if God sends me to the missions, then God will protect me from harm. I have nothing to fear." I was only in the missions for about a month when I realized that I had put words into God's mouth. God never said He would protect me from harm. Better people than me had been murdered in the missions, including St. Oscar Romero and four members of the Cleveland Mission Team. Why would I think that I deserved greater protection than people holier than me? I probably told myself this in order to have the courage to get on the plane. Yet, reflecting on the original calling, I never heard this message. I trust the Lord, but that does not mean bad things cannot happen. We are not in Heaven, yet. I had to humbly accept that I put words into God's mouth so that I would hear what I wanted to hear.

I now had to consider what it meant to be called to the missions in a new, more frightening light. According to Holy Indifference, I now had to accept the possibility that God was going to let me die in the missions. It was at that point that I began to say the prayer I recite every time I am going for a flight: "Lord, if today is the day to die, forgive me my sins and comfort my family. If You should grant me one more day, may it be for Your glory. Amen." Jesus tells us that we should consider carefully the consequences of *letting the Holy Spirit drive*. He says, "Which of you wishing to construct a tower does not first sit down and calculate the cost to see if there is enough for its completion? Otherwise, after laying the foundation and finding himself unable to finish the work, the onlookers should laugh at him and say, 'This one began to build but did not have the resources to finish.'"[15] If we are open to the Divine Plan, we may be asked to sacrifice or even die.

When I was 17 years old, I fell deeply in love with a girl I thought I would marry. The problem was that she was an exchange student from Spain. This is the reason I learned Spanish, which would serve my priesthood very well. Such is Divine Providence. However, the long-distance relationship was too much for us to maintain. A few years later, at age 21, I entered the seminary. As I was packing my belongings into the car to head off to the campus, my ex-girlfriend called me. It had been years since we had spoken. She told me that she had just moved to New York. Compared to Madrid, this sounded like she was right next door. I covered the phone and looked up at the sky and said, "This is so not funny, God. Make up Your mind! I'm about to go to the seminary, and now this phone call?!" I made plans to drive to New York on fall break and visit my

---

[15] Luke 14:28-30 (NAB).

ex-girlfriend. I kept it a secret and continued with my plans to go to the seminary for the fall semester.

For some reason that I still do not understand, I missed the class pictures for the vocation poster. The rector of the seminary, unaware of my plans to go to New York, told me that I needed to go to the studio before I left for fall break. With my car packed for my trip to New York, I stopped by the studio on the way out of town.

There was a deacon who was in charge of taking my picture. It was accomplished very quickly, and then the deacon decided to give me a tour of the studio. I was polite, though uninterested, as I followed him deeper into the back of the studio. He did not even seem to be making much of an effort to show me around. I began to get nervous that things were not as they seemed.

The deacon then sat down in a chair and admitted that he was really trying to get me alone because he had a message from God. He told me that he felt awkward telling me this, but he had learned that ignoring a message from God often made his life miserable. When he heard that only one seminarian missed taking the picture for the poster, he had a deep feeling that God had a reason for it. Obedient to the prompting, he wanted to pray with me a certain type of prayer he had used many times before. He pointed to an empty chair right in front of me and asked if I was willing to pray with him.

All of this was very new and strange to me. I was very uncomfortable. I tried to be polite and explain that I was in a rush, and I would rather just be on my way. The deacon said, "Well, I understand. As I said, I'm a little embarrassed when God asks me to do these things. It sounds hokey. But, I did my part, and that was to invite you to pray. That's all I was supposed to do. By the way, God told me in my prayer that you are going to visit a 'loved one.' He said that you are not to go unless you pray with me. I don't know what that means, but maybe it means something to you." I was stunned! No one knew! Thinking perhaps it was a lucky guess, I decided this guy was not going to ruin my trip to New York. So I agreed, with a grunt and clear annoyance, to do the prayer.

The deacon began with simple words asking the Holy Spirit to be present and speak to us. Then he got very quiet. My eyes were closed, as he had instructed. In the silence, my mind was wandering. I did not tell the deacon what I saw in my imagination. There was a canyon with a river down the middle. People were waving to a boat. On the boat were the pope and some other people. I was sitting on a cliff, overlooking the scene. The deacon, not knowing what I was envisioning, asked, "Is Jesus there?" Up to that point, I had not noticed Jesus in my mind's eye, but now I discovered He was sitting next to me. It was a clever suggestion that I integrated into my imagination.

All I said was, "Yes. He's sitting with me."

The deacon asked, "Is he saying anything?"

A bit resistant to the power of suggestion, I said, "No." And we got quiet again.

In my mind, I suddenly saw someone stand up from the crowd and shoot the Holy Father! The scene repeated in my mind, over and over again. Sometimes, I was in the place of the Holy Father, feeling the bullet pierce my forehead and my head snapping back. Right when the bullet reached me, the deacon, unaware of what I was imagining, touched my head. I jumped, only to find that the deacon was still praying with his eyes closed. Cautiously, I closed my eyes again and returned to the image of the assassination of the pope.

In my mind's eye, Jesus turned to me and said, "Would you die for Me?" As soon as He said this, the deacon said out loud, though he knew nothing of what I was imagining, "Would you die for Him?" I started sobbing and repeating, "Yes, Lord! I give You my life! It is Yours!"

The deacon simply made the Sign of the Cross and ended the prayer. He did not ask me anything or explain anything.

My reaction was strong. I jumped out of the chair and asked, "What was that?! Was that hypnosis?!" Before the deacon had a chance to respond, I muttered something and left the building.

As I opened the car door, I looked up at the sky and yelled, "What was that all about?!" For the next ten hours as I drove to New York, the experience haunted me. Slowly, its meaning came to light. God was asking me if I would give up all my other plans, the whole life I once dreamed of, to follow a new plan, His Plan. And I said "Yes." I meant it, too. Christ talked about someone not being worthy to follow Him, 'No one who sets a hand to the plow and looks to what was left behind is fit for the kingdom of God'".[16] I had to let go of the past and focus on the new direction God had given me. If I was to join myself to the Church as a clergyman, I would have to let my other dreams die.

When I arrived in New York, I told my ex-girlfriend the entire story of the deacon. She responded, "You're not coming back to me, are you?" I shook my head from side to side. My eyes were filled with

---

[16] Luke 9:62 (NAB).

tears, but they were not for her. I was so touched that God had affirmed my vocation in such a powerful way. I felt unworthy of such love and attention. He was calling me, and I would give everything for Him.

I relay this story to help you realize what it means to enter into communication with God. It means that we are willing to let the Holy Spirit drive. With Holy Indifference, we give God Veto Power to direct our lives. As we Purify Our Prayer, we realize that God knows best what will make us happy and fulfilled. We must consider the cost of discipleship and humbly accept our weaknesses and our need for a Savior. Trust the Lord!

I strongly encourage those I spiritually direct to keep their **Spiritual Radar** on and tuned. Pay attention to the ways God may be communicating with you through various promptings. Note the events that seem like a pattern or a strange coincidence. Note the internal movements of your heart. Note the moments when you feel drawn toward or away from a decision. Take time to consciously listen for anything the Lord might want to communicate with you. What a blessed existence we have to walk with our Lord. We always want Christ to pay attention to us; do we not owe Christ the same courtesy? So as not to "freak us out," those promptings of the Holy Spirit may be soft and gentle, so we must intentionally look for them. Keep your Spiritual Radar on.

C. S. Lewis gave a wonderful analogy of a **Wartime Radio,** which I will expand upon.[17] The static of the radio crackles as the family

---

[17] C.S. Lewis, *Mere Christianity* (New York: Macmillian Publishing Co., Inc., 1952), 51.

huddles around it, slowly tuning it, seeking a signal. Suddenly, a voice can be heard. “To all of you behind enemy lines: Take courage! We are winning the war! The enemy is retreating. Endure the challenges. Your Savior is fast approaching. Stay tuned for further instructions. You, too, can help the cause!” Perhaps in this world, our lines of communication are filled with static. Still, there are moments, ever so briefly, when we hear the Good News. It motivates and directs us to do our part “for the cause.”

THE LITTLE FLOWER

One devotion of my family is the **Prayer of St. Thérèse, the Little Flower**. Our tradition has been to make a request to God and ask St. Thérèse to intercede. Say twenty-four Glory Be’s each day for twenty-four days. In that time, if you receive a rose, St. Thérèse is letting you know that your prayer was granted. What I like about this prayer is that it makes no demands. I am not saying the prayers in order to receive something. I am merely giving glory to God while being alert to any communication from my dear friend, St. Thérèse. If I do not get a rose, it does not mean that the prayer failed. It simply means that the answer was “no” or the answer is not mine to know. I trust the Lord. I make my petition known while I leave the decision entirely to God.

I have used this prayer many times in my life. Only twice have I received a rose. Once was when I was asking God if I should build a school in El Salvador. On the 24th day of my prayers, hundreds of roses bloomed, a month early, outside of my window. I built the school.

The second time I received a rose was when a woman I was spiritually directing was suffering from insomnia for over two years. Her physical and mental health were critical. As I began to lose hope that she would survive, I asked God if I should expect a healing miracle. The odds were against it. One morning, there was a vase of two dozen roses on my dining room table. In an unprecedented manner, a group that, unbeknownst to me, had used my house for a meeting, uncharacteristically bought roses and decided to leave them in the rectory. They had no idea I was doing the Prayer of St. Thérèse. Despite her not believing my story, a few weeks later, the woman I was praying for was cured! Maybe you have your own prayers. This prayer is part of our great Tradition. Use what we got, I say!

A warning about prayer requests: **Do Not Test the Lord**. It is insulting to the Lord to try to make deals regarding moral or prudent behavior. It is improper to say, "Lord, if You do this (fill in the blank), then I will do this (fill in the blank) which I am already supposed to do, but I would rather not." For example, "If I win this next hand of Blackjack, then I will try to smooth things over with my wife." Or, "If my brother comes over and repays me the money he owes me, I'll invite him to the wedding." The idea is that we are bargaining with Jesus concerning our faithfulness. We are claiming that we would be good disciples if the Lord would be more faithful with our requests first. Equally problematic is when we take unnecessary, sometimes dangerous risks under the guise that we are "trusting the Lord." We do not drink and drive, hang out with gang members, or take out loans we cannot afford and say, "I trust the Lord." We are merely trying to force the Lord to do something, while threatening to call Him unfaithful if He does not do as we wish. Do Not Test the Lord! Be prudent. Be responsible. Be reverent. Be faithful.

Take very seriously any promptings or communications that you have discerned to be authentically Divine in origin. If God speaks, we must listen. It would be better to blindly stumble down the path of life than to clearly hear the Voice of God and ignore Him. "If you deny Me before others, I will deny you before My Heavenly Father,"[18] says the Lord. For this reason, the Lord will be far more lenient to the pagans who have not known His ways than to us who have received so much. "I tell you, many prophets and righteous people longed to see what you see, but did not see it."[19] That is why the gift of communication with God should be received with gratitude and seriousness.

---

[18] Matthew 10:33 (NAB).

[19] Matthew 3:17a (NAB).

Chapter 4

We Seem to Have a Bad Signal: God's Ambiguity

WHY AREN'T YOU LISTENING?

One of the frustrations people have with prayer is that they often feel they are not being heard. When we feel a petition is not granted, we feel like God was not listening. On one level, we all know that God is not a genie or a waiter who takes your order and, poof! there you go. The goal, of course, is to learn how to love, trust, and follow Christ. But instead of seeking this goal, we, like St. Peter, try to tell Jesus the way things ought to be.[1] Obviously, we want to conform

[1] Matthew 16:23 (NAB).

our will and desires to God's great plan. We believe that God loves us, that God is good, and that God's plan is good, even when it does not seem to match our plans. That being said, it is not only acceptable to make our petitions to the Lord, but He wants us to "knock and the door will be opened."[2] So, we make our requests and wait for the response.

Still, we are often frustrated that the Lord did not answer a request. We feel silly continuing to ask the same thing over and over again. Or, when the opposite of our request happens, we wonder if any of our prayers are worth uttering. One of the spiritual direction techniques that I use when people are frustrated with their prayers seemingly not being answered is called "**Purifying Your Prayer**." The concept of purifying your prayer came to me in one of those powerful moments of prayer when the Lord spoke so clearly to me. It was not words, but I understood. The best way I can describe what He said to me was, "Every prayer that has ever been uttered has been answered in my Son, Jesus Christ." I was on fire with this Truth, though I did not understand it at first.

Upon further reflection, I wondered if that message made any sense. Certainly, I have prayed for things that God did not answer. I realized that, underneath every prayer, there are certain deeper desires that must be understood. Under those desires, there are still deeper desires. This continues until we find the deepest desire and fulfillment in Christ. For example, I might pray to win the lottery. But do I really want the lottery? Really, I want the money. But why?

---

[2] Matthew 7:7b (NAB).

So I can buy things that will make me comfortable and happy, develop my dreams, be charitable and important, be secure in my future, with no worries about financial woes. So, what I really want is to be comfortable, happy, fulfilled, generous, important, and secure. Comfort, of course, is more about not having pain or worries. If I am fulfilled, then I will be happy. If I am generous, I will feel good about myself, which makes me important. So, I really want to be free of pain and worries, be fulfilled, and be good. As I continue, I find that the deeper I go, the more I realize that Christ is offering me my deepest desires. He is offering me the chance to live with Him in heaven, in perfect paradise, without pain, death, fear, worries, or even tears. He is showing me the way to please His Divine Heart, which makes me more fulfilled and important than the applause from anyone else in all of history. With His grace, He will make me a holy Saint, with virtue and meaning in my life. Every prayer that has ever been uttered has been answered in the Person of Jesus Christ!

Another derivation of the Purifying Prayer is offered by St. Ignatius of Loyola. He suggests evaluating one of the many fantasies we all have.[3] In your fantasy, how do you see yourself? Is this who you really want to be? What do you desire in your fantasy? What is the deeper, truer desire? What can you do in real life to become that person you really want to be and achieve that goal you truly desire?

---

[3] Hampton Wright, Vinita. "Finding God in Our Desires." Ignatian Spirituality, July 13, 2023. https://www.ignatianspirituality.com/finding-god-in-our-desires/.

Christopher West, a theologian of *Theology of the Body*, gives a witness about a vision he had:[4] The women in the office were looking out the window gawking over some construction workers that were not wearing shirts. He thought to himself that he would like it if women would look at him that way. Then, he had a vision. He was standing on the beach. A handsome man with big muscles and a girl on each arm walked by him and smiled. Then another man came down the beach: beaten, bloody, with a Crown of Thorns, and dragging a Cross. Jesus stopped in front of Christopher and said, "Who is the Real Man?" His fantasy (or vision) became a realization of a much deeper, more meaningful desire.

Sometimes we struggle with the reality that life seems so unfair and difficult. Either we experience it personally, or we witness others who are suffering. We want to believe that God, who is all-powerful, is good and loving. Yet, the fact that bad things happen to good people is troubling. There are the patented, theological answers that God sees good results beyond the seemingly unfair tragedy, or that the cause of suffering is all the sinners in the world. I never found these responses to be very comforting. For spiritual direction, I think it is best to recognize that life and suffering are unfair. Why does God not do something about it? I do not have the answer. We must be honest with those we direct. We give them what has been revealed and not merely our speculation or the answers that help us put the question out of our minds. There is something healthy and holy about wrestling with the tough questions.

---

[4] Christopher West, *Good News About Sex and Marriage Revised Edition* (Cincinnati, OH: Servant Books, 2004), 159.

I have a lot of questions to ask God when I see Him. I do know that God loves us. If we love someone, we rejoice when our loved one rejoices, and we suffer when our loved one suffers. Jesus is crying with us in our distress. Maybe the answer is as simple as, "This is not heaven, but my heart longs to be there." It matters to me that Jesus feels my pain and anguish, even if I do not understand why He lets it happen. This is the moment I learn how to trust Him when I do not know the answers.

We often focus on the moments we think that God is not doing His job the right way. In itself, this statement should make us laugh and become a little more humble. At the same time, there are probably lots of ways God has blessed and protected us that we may never realize, which I will call "**Anonymous Intervention**." Did you know that the enormous planet Jupiter, with its powerful gravity, gobbles up the vast majority of meteorites that were heading toward Earth? How many times has God saved humanity simply by giving us Jupiter? St. Thérèse of Lisieux reflected on this invisible protection that must constantly be occurring. In a simplified way, St. Therese explains: If a young girl ran into the garden and tripped on a stone that was out of place, she might fall and injure herself. She would call to her father, and he would come and make her feel better. Then, she would know her father's love. But what if her father went to the garden before she arrived? Perhaps he would notice the stone out of place and think, 'I better put that where it belongs so my little girl doesn't get hurt.' Then the young girl would run into the garden, never tripping, never falling, never getting hurt, never calling out to her father, and never knowing her father's love because he never needed to rescue her and make her feel better. Clearly the second scenario was the more loving, though she was unaware of it. Thérèse continues writing something like: "How many times has my heavenly Father protected me and cleared the stones from my path without me ever knowing? Thank you for loving me so dearly, my Jesus."[5]

Now that we have accepted that we do not know in what way our prayers will be answered, we might feel a bit anxious. We can rest assured that God is busy loving us, but we cannot avoid the occasional suffering that is part of our lives prior to entering heaven. Those anxieties are not insanity or a lack of trust in the Lord. It is normal to be aware of how vulnerable and fragile we are. Though we have the guarantee of God's mercy, we have no guarantee that we will be spared earthly suffering. So what do we do with these anxieties?

Our Lord tells us not to worry. He points to the birds that make their nests, explaining that they have nothing to worry about since God has provided the materials and knowledge of nest-building. Yet, you are much more precious to God than a bird.[6] God knows every hair on your head. We are called to trust in a way that feels unnatural and counterintuitive. After all, look at what happened to the martyrs, or Jesus on the Cross! Yet, worries are not very helpful, and can even be an impediment to doing the difficult things God is asking us to do. How should we rid ourselves of such worries without becoming so naïve as to imagine nothing bad can happen to us?

---

[5] Therese of Lisieux, *Story of a Soul: The Autobiography of St. Therese of Lisieux*, trans. John Clarke (Washington, D.C.: Institute of Carmelite Studies Publications, 1976), 84.

[6] Matthew 6:26 (NAB).

In spiritual direction, I teach a mental exercise to help manage our worldly anxieties. Here, of course, I am not referring to the type of anxiety that needs to be diagnosed and treated by a professional in psychology. I am referring to the ordinary, daily worries that people carry with them. This exercise is called "**Presenting My Worries.**" I ask the person to imagine a basket in front of the tabernacle, monstrance, or in a prayer space. Name the worries. Imagine that each worry is a physical object that you are placing in the basket. Once you have named them all and placed them in the basket, mentally slide the basket to Jesus. Say a little prayer that you need Christ's help with these worries. Now, you can just talk to the Lord. You already talked about the anxieties, so pray about everything else. Let the conversation with your Lord develop with His grace. Leave those worries out of it. Sometimes we just need a rest from our worries. They weigh heavy on us all day long. When you are done praying, let Jesus slide the basket back to you. I know you do not want to accept the worries, but you are going to have to pick up some of them. However, you do not need them all. Just pick up the objects that Jesus wants to give you. These are your duties, the people you are asked to care for, and the important decisions that have to be made. Leave the rest. Many burdens are not ours to carry. Leave them with Jesus. They are in His hands now. Remember the ***Serenity Prayer***: Lord, grant me the serenity to accept the things I cannot change, the courage to change the things I can, and the wisdom to know the difference. Amen.

I know that some people want to leave all of their worries in God's hands. There may be some things that God is placing on your heart, causing you to feel the pressure to do something about it.

Practically speaking, there are some worries that give us stress simply because they are our responsibilities. In Bobby McFerrin's song, "*Don't Worry. Be Happy*," there is a line that says, "The landlord say your rent is late. He may have to litigate," but "don't worry, be happy."[7] That is terrible advice. We must take care of our duties, even if it stresses us out at times. Otherwise, we use prayer as a form of **escapism**. We pretend that we are holy because God has taken into His hands all of our responsibilities. Instead, use this prayer method to help know the difference between what God is asking you to accept as your responsibility, and what you now can leave behind. You cannot be very effective if you carry too many burdens. Manage your stress appropriately, and let God be a part of that decision.

As we grow in our comfort with prayer, we move from more proper and formal language to a more genuine expression of our true feelings. We might pray, "Lord, highest glory belongs to You. May Your holy will be accomplished through the grace You give me." On other occasions, you might pray, "Lord, I think it's really lousy that You couldn't let me get through just two traffic lights! Is that too much to ask?! Now I'm late, and I feel foolish. Thanks a lot!" The second prayer seems more genuine. That is what we are feeling, at times. However, I advise you to remember with Whom you are talking! God deserves love and respect. Be genuine, but be reverent. If we become too casual in our prayer life, we may begin to treat God as just another person. God can tolerate our moody prayers, but we

---

[7] "Don't Worry, Be Happy," track 1 on Bobby McFerrin, *Simple Pleasures*, Capitol Records, 1988.

need to condition our hearts to be more aware of our right relationship with him. Be authentic, but humble.

It is true that we do not have to be in a church to pray. We can pray while sitting, driving, showering, etc. Yet, there is some value in occasionally getting down on one's knees. Jesus does not need me to kneel in a church in order to pray; I need to kneel in a church in order to remember to pray reverently. We call this virtue or spiritual gift, "**Fear of the Lord**." We are not "afraid," because we know God is a loving Father. Yet, we are aware God deserves our respect.

JUST TELL ME WHAT TO DO!

From Hollywood movies, we are familiar with the spiritual warfare term known as "possession." The idea is that a person is controlled by demonic forces that steal away his freedom to choose to be holy and healthy. While pop culture prefers to focus on the demonic aspect, I think it is more productive to focus on free will.

Free will is a theological term that St. Thomas Aquinas teaches is a fundamental and essential aspect of humanity.[8] We are free to make choices in our lives. Obviously, we are not free to choose to breathe underwater or fly without the required gear. There are parameters around our choices. At the same time, out of all the creatures in the universe, we appear to be the only ones capable of choosing to sin.

Obviously, the gift of free will was not given to us in order for us to sin. God does permit us to sin, but He does not want us to sin.

---

[8] Thomas Aquinas, *Summa Theologiae*, I, Q. 83, Art. 1.

It would seem that free will has another purpose, namely, that free will is a necessary ingredient for love. Here, "love" is not a mere emotion; it is a decision to place the good of the other person above our own good. In order for love to be authentic, it must be freely offered.

As mentioned previously, love requires a level of freedom. You cannot force someone to love you. The ability to genuinely love seems to be reserved for humans. We are invited to use our free will to respond to God's love with love.

God will not force us to love Him. God gives us the freedom to choose to love Him. This means that God must give us the option not to love Him. If I say, "We have three options for lunch: burgers, burgers, or burgers," then we really do not have a choice. There must be at least one other option to call it a "choice." So, if God gives us a choice to love Him, the alternative option is not to love, which is to sin. If God does not permit sin, then God has taken away our choice. Without choice, we have no freedom. Without our freedom, we cannot love.

In the case of possession, a person loses the ability to choose. He is controlled by demonic forces. God does not operate this way. God will never control us. Ever so gently, God invites us to participate in and respond to His love.

One of my spiritual principles is that **God is Gentle**. Because God is so powerful and awesome, and we are so small and fragile, God must be extremely gentle with us. If I speak to a child, I must be careful of my tone and demeanor. If I sincerely want the child to share her thoughts or make her own decisions, I must be careful not to manipulate or intimidate her. I might gently guide the conversation in a sort of Socratic Method, but I have to be very cautious not to use my authority or size to take away her sincerity or freedom of choice. So it is with God. I believe that God gently offers us indications of His holy desire without forcing our decisions.

This is one of the reasons why God can appear to be ambiguous in communicating with us. I certainly have argued with God that it would be better if I heard a booming voice from the heavens tell me what to do, but this very rarely happens. Even with God's whispers in my heart, they are so infrequent and soft that I often miss them. Only on reflection do I recognize that God had been guiding or prompting me at all. God does not want to take away our freedom. God invites us, but then He lets us choose the way to respond. God will never "possess" us. Love does not allow for possession.

Another spiritual principle is that **God Does Not Micromanage.** God expects us to make decisions, be creative, and add our fingerprints to the artwork. We are co-authoring the plan for tomorrow. It is an awesome privilege and responsibility. God does not want us to sit back and watch Him do it all. If that were the Divine Plan, why make us at all? Why give us free will? Jesus said, "I no longer call you slaves. A slave does not know what his master is doing. I call you friends. I have told you everything the Father has told me."[9] "You are my friends if you do what I command you." [10] "Do you love Me? Feed My sheep."[11] Christ is calling us to actively participate in His Plan, though the instructions are intentionally vague. It may

---

[9] John 15:15b (NAB).

[10] John 15:14 (NAB).

[11] See John 21:17 (NAB).

seem frightful to wield such power, but, so long as we are open to Christ's intervention in our lives, we have a safety net. The Holy Spirit will put us back on the right track if we stray too far. I call this **God's Veto Power**. At any time, I give God permission to veto my decisions, and I will abandon my plans for His. Because of this, I need to keep my spiritual radar on the ready for any communication from the Lord.

STAR OF BETHLEHEM

We are called to be vigilant always.[12] That is because we never know when God is going to call upon us. We must keep our spiritual radar on and be checking in with the Lord often just in case there is a message. Though we might want the answers immediately, God's timing is perfect.

I have often considered that the star that led the wise men to the newborn Jesus[13] was a spectacular celestial invitation that must have been millions of years in the making. At the right moment, the stars (or probably planets) would line up so as to become significant to these men who spent their nights studying the sky. Given the astronomical physics and the amount of time it takes for planets to travel those distances, think about how long ago God must have been planning this moment. Did God make the plan during the Big Bang? Or did God give a little nudge to an asteroid to begin the dominoes effect that led to this event? Or did God change the order of the galaxy to accommodate His great plan? Thus it is with **God's Timing**. God

[12] See Matthew 24:42 (NAB).

[13] Matthew 2:1 (NAB).

knows exactly when to intervene and when not to intervene in order to fulfill His Plan of Salvation. When the Lord is quiet, trust God's timing.

COMFORTABLE WITH VAGUENESS

When we are discerning between two options, both being good, it is appropriate to ask God which He prefers. God may have some greater plan. Hopefully, the discernment process will reveal that preference. If we are attentive, then we should be able to recognize the gentle promptings of the Lord leading us toward one option over another.

At other times, God may not have a preference. Either choice might serve His Will. Perhaps the greatest good comes from our choosing. It can feel frustrating when we do not perceive any guidance or response from God. This may simply mean the choice is left to us. Yet, the more important question within the discernment process is: Why do we choose one option over another? Is it for God's glory? Or have we allowed other, less noble factors to interfere with our choice? I believe it pleases the Lord when we take seriously the discernment process so as to purify our intentions and, honestly and earnestly, seek to serve the Divine Will.

When we are diligent in making decisions through prayer and discernment, we should have a certain confidence without being arrogant. We may make mistakes, but the mistakes will never be so bad as to thwart the Divine Plan. If we are honest in our discernment, God will guide us. If we begin down a path that does not serve

God's Will, He will let us know. We can trust that the Lord will never abandon us.

One thing that sometimes frustrates me and sometimes makes me marvel is when I sense that God is prompting me toward a certain decision, but He does not explain the purpose or the goal. One afternoon, I was sitting in a pool overhearing a conversation. They mentioned the African nation of Ghana. When I heard the word, "Ghana," it rang funny in my heart. I thought perhaps it was nothing more than indigestion. A few weeks later, someone else brought up Ghana. I asked why he said, "Ghana," and he claimed they were trying to name a random country. I thought, "Random? Maybe." This pattern repeated many times over the years, though I could not understand why. I had no experience or knowledge of Ghana. I did not know anyone from Ghana. I would have trouble finding Ghana on a map.

Several months later, I was told by the diocese that a missionary was assigned to speak at my parish. As it turns out, he had served in Ghana. I finally decided that this must be a Prompting of the Holy Spirit. I said a prayer, "Okay, God. I'm not sure what you are trying to say, but I hear you talking about Ghana. I will visit Ghana if you so desire, but I cannot just get on a plane and show up in a random country. You will need to provide me with a contact. Otherwise, I will assume that this prompting is for some other reason."

Within an hour, my cousin, who was the Provincial General for the Holy Cross Priests, called me. Unfortunately, his sister had passed away, and he was coming into town and asked for some assistance with the funeral Mass. I agreed and casually asked where he was calling from. He said, "Ghana."

I responded, "Of course you are… Why are you in Ghana?" He explained that, as Provincial General, he had to visit the Holy Cross community in Ghana. Realizing that my prayer had just been answered, I made arrangements to visit Ghana and have the Holy Cross priests give me transportation and lodging.

I went to Ghana without knowing what to expect. Fortunately, the residents speak English, so communication was not an issue. I had no specific purpose for my trip and simply waited for God to let me know what I was supposed to do or who I was supposed to encounter. After the ten day visit, I came home, just as puzzled as when I left.

The experience was beautiful, but I still do not know why God had me visit Ghana. Perhaps there was some part of the Divine Plan that I had inadvertently fulfilled. Perhaps it had nothing to do with me, but, in some way, I had influenced someone else. Perhaps there is still a piece to this puzzle that has not yet been revealed to me. Though I could speculate a million reasons, honestly, I simply do not know. Yet, I have to believe that there is value in just being willing to go where Jesus sends me. Though I may never understand the purpose of my trip, I pray that God is pleased that I was obedient. May it be for the glory of God.

I feel it is necessary to point out that, while we take God's communication very seriously, I still believe that God sends us little blessings that are not intended to change the paths of our lives. They are just messages of love. I call them, "**Kisses From Heaven**." An elderly woman after Mass waved to me to come over to her. She then grabbed my hand and pulled me down to her face and kissed me. I asked, "What was that for?" She said, "To show my affection for you, of course." We should not over-analyze every aspect of our lives as being a significant, life-changing, earth-shattering event. Sometimes, I think God just wants to shower us with kisses for no other reason than to show us affection. It is the parking spot that opened up right when you needed it, or the falling cup of coffee that landed in such a way as not to spill, or the perfect person to happen to walk into the room when you needed her, or the diagnosis that was not as bad as you thought. There are a million times a day we should say, "Thank You, Lord." Does that mean that God has been following you around, doing extra favors for you today that He does not do on other days or for other people? Why would God do that? Maybe, it is just in our minds, a series of coincidences. Or maybe they are kisses from Heaven. In any event, it is a good reminder of God's love and affection, even if it was just a fluke event.

GOD'S PRIORITIES

For many of the decisions of our lives, the consequences are relatively immediate. We eat, and we have energy. We diet, and we lose weight. We leave late for work, and we annoy our employer with our tardiness. Other decisions are more long term: We delay instant gratification for bigger goals, like retirement. We work hard in school to get a job that pays well. We learn a foreign language that will be used throughout a professional career.

Setting our priorities helps us to endure sacrificing the immediate benefits for the sake of the long-term goal. Yet, even here, our priorities can become unbalanced. We might set a long-term goal of sending our children to college. We make the sacrifice of working long hours and foregoing personal time and vacations. At some point, we begin to sacrifice our family time. Though college is important, children having involved parents is important too. What would it matter if a child could go to college if she never knew the love of her parents?

Jesus puts it this way: "What profit is there for one to gain the whole world and forfeit his life?"[14] In other words, we are called to get our priorities in order. Spiritual direction can be a useful tool in setting and balancing goals according to our priorities. However, it should be noted that "God's ways are not our ways."[15] God's priorities are not always our priorities.

Because of this difference in priorities, we often complain that God is not doing His job properly. "God, why didn't You intervene?" "Everything would have worked out if You would've just prevented this one thing from happening." "Everything is lost because You didn't make other people go along with the plan." The truth is that God is looking at a much longer timeline than we are. God is thinking about the priorities of eternity. We, rightfully, place great importance in the work that we are doing since it is, presumably, the work that God has given us to accomplish. Yet, the success of the task may not be the final objective the Lord is aiming to achieve. Our failure may be part of the plan. God's plan is constantly focused on the salvation of humanity. Though God loves each of us individually and appreciates every hair of our heads and every breath that we breathe and all the effort that we offer for His glory, the priorities of

---

[14] Mark 8:36 (NAB).

[15] Isaiah 55:8b (NAB).

God are not always the same as ours. Letting God lead means that, if we are faithful, we must trust that our efforts, even our failures, will serve the Lord.

Chapter 5

Freedom to Follow the Lord

You have to admire St. Peter and the other apostles who could drop their nets and follow Jesus at a moment's notice.[1] Nothing impeded them. Nothing was going to get in the way of this great opportunity. They seem far freer than most of us who claim to live in the "Land of the Free." We tend to be bogged down with commitments, expectations, mortgages, personal plans, and even spiritual obstacles that prevent us from leaving everything and following.

All of us have experienced the phenomenon in which we want to do what is right and holy, but we end up choosing the sin instead. St. Paul talks about the frustration caused when he does the things he does not want to do while not doing the things he does want to

[1] Matthew 4:20 (NAB).

do.[2] Using the Ignatian *Examen*[3] can help reveal how often this happens in our lives. We intend to be patient with someone, but reflect afterward that we were not. We intend to be diligent in our work, but reflect later that we wasted time. We intend to have only one drink, but reflect that we drank too much.

We have all experienced the frustration of giving advice to people who do not even see the possibility of living holy lives. Instead, they insist that they have no choice but to be resentful, unfaithful, fraudulent, manipulative, violent, or inclined to any other sin that is not going to lead to happiness. If we are to serve the Lord with all of our hearts, minds, and souls, we must free ourselves from those things that impede our ability to follow Him. Freedom is a great gift, but it is a gift we can lose if we are not careful.

Sometimes people experience what are known as spiritual "attachments" or "obsessions." These spiritual realities have usually been freely chosen and/or fostered with bad habits. Attachments diminish a person's ability to make good choices. We have an inward attraction, disdain, habits, expectation or blindness that pulls them toward one option over others.. Rather than looking at the facts and listening to the promptings of the Lord, we follow a way of thinking that leads us to an incorrect conclusion or an unwise decision. It is similar to what sociologists refer to "confirmation bias": If a doctor assumes the patient is has a kidney stone, he or she will look for symptoms that match that hypothesis. In the process, the doctor

---

[2] Romans 7:15b (NAB).

[3] Ignatius of Loyola, *The Text of the Spiritual Exercises of Saint Ignatius*, 13.

tends to overlook the other symptoms or indicators that would lead to the true diagnosis.

Attachments are feelings of a certain connection to some belief or influence that is not of God.[4] Think of people who have occasional thoughts of prejudice. They do not believe in prejudices as truthful or good, yet they struggle to rid themselves of these tendencies. Where a temptation may be a fleeting thought, an attachment is a reoccurring, incorrect, way of thinking. In learning the piano, it does not help if you practice the wrong notes over and over again. Attachment is the wrong way of thinking repeated to the point of becoming a reflexive, "go-to" response. If I find that a person is suffering from a spiritual attachment, I use routine prayer to help reorient the mind and heart toward the things of God. A daily *Examen* may help a person recognize these attachments and begin to work toward freedom.

If a person is struggling with spiritual **Obsession**, they have incessant thoughts that are contrary to God or to the reality that God has revealed.[5] Though they may sincerely believe in the Lord's teachings and revelations, they struggle to be free from the lies that are deeply rooted in their consciousness. For example, a person may struggle to shake the feeling that he or she is unworthy of God's love. Another person might have resentments or jealousies that steal away

---

[4] John of the Cross, *John of the Cross: Selected Writings*, ed. and trans. Kieran Kavanaugh (Mahwah, NJ: Paulist Press, 1987), 65.

[5] Kathleen Beckman, *A Family Guide to Spiritual Warfare: Strategies for Deliverance and Healing* (Manchester, NH: Sophia Institute Press, 2020), 100-102.

the sense of peace. They are aware that they are stuck on a false belief, but feel powerless to change it. It does not, necessarily, cause a person to actively choose sinful actions, but it paralyzes them with fear and anxiety so that they are unable to engage in the good that God calls us to live. In psychology, they may refer to a sense of being unable to free one's self from false beliefs as a type of obsessive-compulsive disorder. That diagnosis would need a professional's opinion. For others, they have momentary back-slides to old ways of thinking that they know are untrue, like a nagging feeling that we are unworthy or that God is an angry God. If these thoughts are not constant or debilitating, they may just be something like an echo of an older way of thinking. However, if the thoughts begin to create barriers in one's life from doing good, it is time to take care of the problem. Spiritual obsession requires more than a prayer routine. It will require deliverance prayers[6] and may include the work of a professional counselor or a trained priest. It is best to work as a team.

SANCTIFYING MEMORIES

Another obstacle that some people face is a traumatic experience that has created an impediment to total commitment and trust of the Lord. The traumatic events in our lives continue to haunt us. We have a hard time moving past them. Though we sometimes quarantine the memories in the back of our minds, they can warp and paralyze our perception of ourselves, of God, or of life. If people were victims of violence, they may have difficulty feeling safe. They

---

[6] Kathleen Beckman, *A Family Guide to Spiritual Warfare*, 203-233.

may have issues with intimacy. They may be unable to handle stress effectively. To be free enough to commit to following the Lord, they need spiritual healing.

I always encourage those dealing with trauma to seek professional counseling. Spiritual direction can work together with psychological therapies to restore peace and integrate the experience into a person's life in a way that is no longer limiting. The method I use to help people process traumatic memories is called **"Sanctifying the Memory."**

When someone has traumatic memories, he or she often replays the memory in his mind, like a movie that is stuck in the same scene. The person experiences the feelings of the original event, causing distress and panic. Sanctifying the Memory begins, as always, with asking the Holy Spirit to guide the experience. Then I ask the person to describe the event that is replaying in his or her mind. It should be noted that the memory continues to morph and change as the person remembers it. There are sights, sounds, and even images that are not necessarily from the actual event, yet they become part of the memory of the event as a type of symbolic representation of the way the trauma feels to the person who experienced it. For example, the man perpetrating the violence might begin to have a devilish appearance in the memory. The victim may see herself as a child, though she was older at the time of the event. After describing whatever the event was as he or she remembers it, ask the questions, "Where is Christ in your memory?"

For most people, it is difficult to find Christ. There may even be some resentment that Christ did not protect them from the trauma. There might be some sense that the trauma was deserved because of their unworthiness in God's eyes. Certain people may even feel that, having experienced the trauma, they are now broken or tainted and no longer able to be intimate with the Lord.

When a person is struggling to find Jesus in the recurring memory, I give the instructions, "Imagine that the memory is being recorded by a television camera. The camera sees the perspective you normally see when the memory replays in your mind. Now, place yourself just outside the actual scene. You are watching the event happen to you as if you are observing an actor playing your part. This helps you to detach yourself from the disturbing emotion. Those emotions can prevent you from perceiving clearly the event. Now, look around the studio. Where is Jesus? He might be just off-camera, just outside of the scene that you have been replaying, but He is definitely there. Find Him. What does He look like? What are the expressions on His face while He watches the scene? Is He saying anything? Is He feeling anything?"

After getting a little feedback, I continue, "Now go talk to Jesus. Let Christ express His feelings and perspective to you. You know Him. You can anticipate His responses. Do you see how much it hurt Christ that you went through what you went through? Do you see how much He desired to take your place? Do you see the wounds on His hands and around His head bleeding a little as He experiences your pain? Do you know that God cares deeply for you? Do you know that you were never alone in your experience? Do you know how much Christ wants to save you and heal you, even now?"

Though Sanctifying the Memory does not give an answer to the question of why God did not intervene, it helps people know that there is someone who understands and compassionately loves them.

They are not alone in those traumatic moments, though it might have felt like they were.

I find that God has always been with me, but I did not always notice. It is often after the events, upon reflection, that I then recognize that God's hand had been guiding me or that Christ had been walking with me. When I returned from the missions, everyone patted me on the back. They claimed to admire me for the good work I did. Yet, the things they would say let me know that they had no clue what I had been through or whether or not I did anything worth complimenting. People say, "You were a missionary? How was that?" I always laugh to myself. What am I supposed to say? Can I sum up the significance of my six years in a few sentences? When I attempt an answer, people usually respond, "Good for you," or "I admire you for that." Then we jump conversations to other people they know who had done trips to foreign lands, or tourist trips they had been on, or politics, or the immediate issues of the day. How could I take seriously their praise? How could I believe that I did a good job?

I entered into prayer. Jesus was in the missions long before I arrived, and Jesus remains there even now. He is, truly, the only one who understands what the experience was like for me. Even the other missionaries each had their own perspectives and personal issues that changed the way they experienced the ministry. Every circumstance was different, and every person handled it differently. Yet, Jesus understands me intimately. He knew how hard it was for me to drop everything I was doing so I could pay attention to the person who just walked up to my door. He knew how hard it was for me to be patient when the night before I hardly slept because the phobia of spiders in my bedroom kept me up all night. He knew how I had to reach down deep to find the courage to face challenges I had never had to deal with before and was certain that I would not handle completely correctly. Jesus is the only one who truly understands my life.

Using the Sanctifying the Memory technique, I walked with Christ through some of the memories of El Salvador that still bothered me. In my mind, He turned to me and said something like, "For the times you fell short of being the best you could have been, I forgive you. You went where I sent you. You did what I asked you to do. You did it the way I asked you to do it. That is enough. I am pleased with you." Hearing those words, even if it was just in my prayer, filled me with such peace. Could I ask for anything more than to please the Lord?

LINGERING SENSE OF GUILT

Sometimes people suddenly remember sins they committed many years ago that they have not thought of in a long time. They are bothered by the **Old Sins Remembered** that occasionally pop into their heads. They cannot remember if they had already confessed the sin. They figure it would have been including with, "For these and all my sins," at the end of their routine confession. So why is it coming to the surface now? To be sure, if it is a mortal sin that has not been confessed, it should be confessed at the earliest opportunity. However, sometimes it is an old spiritual wound that has healed but there remains some irritation.

Most priests simply say that this has already been forgiven. Sometimes they scold the person for doubting God's forgiveness. I prefer to consider this as a wound that still needs further healing. Though God has, undoubtedly, forgiven the person (if the mortal sins were confessed), the sin continues to affect the sinner's perspective and inclinations. A person may have confessed a sexual sin of his adolescence but continue to have issues with chastity. It has been my experience that we are most fortified against a particular temptation when we have never committed that sin. It is so much easier to sin a second time when we have already fallen in the past. It is easier to resist the first drink than the second. It is easier to justify cheating on a spouse the second time. Once we view ourselves as fallen, we are not as careful to protect our holiness. Though we have been forgiven for the specific sins of our past, these choices may have opened the door to a long pattern of sinful behavior or inclinations.

Perhaps God places these memories of old sins on the heart of the penitent with the desire to offer healing; to renew the person, starting with the origin of the wound. It is better to simply offer forgiveness and pray for healing than to argue about whether or not someone has already been forgiven. That person still feels the wound. Bring the remedy of God's mercy.

At the same time, it is not uncommon for people to have difficulty letting themselves be healed. Though they may not doubt the mercy of God, they doubt their own worthiness for such a gift. They continue to punish themselves and belittle their own dignity based on a sin that God has already forgiven. I wonder if this is what Christ meant when He said, "Every sin and blasphemy will be forgiven, but blasphemy against the Spirit will not be forgiven."[7] I interpret this as being our acceptance, or lack thereof, of the power of the Holy Spirit to forgive us. God does not force His love upon us. He offers forgiveness; it is up to us to accept or refuse it.

It can be a type of scrupulosity, which is an obsessive pattern of thinking that debilitates a person from moving past their mistakes. It can also be a type of pride to believe that there exists some type of sin that could be more powerful than God's mercy. How can it be that your sin is worse than any other sin in history? How can you think so highly of your own power as to believe you could do anything that God could not immediately undo? Either way of thinking, scrupulosity or pride, is in need of healing by the appropriate expert.

One exercise I use to point out the great power of Christ's mercy is to go through a logical sequence called, **The Worst Sin**. It goes like this: Stealing is wrong. Stealing food from a friend is worse. Stealing food from a starving prisoner is worse. Killing the prisoner to steal his food is worse. Killing an orphan to steal his food is worse. Killing an orphan for no reason is worse. Killing the son of the president is worse. Killing your own son is worse. Torturing and killing your son is worse. Torturing and killing the only Son of God, who was innocent and wanted only to love us, is the worst sin ever! And yet, from the Cross, Christ forgave us.[8] How can we be so arrogant as to think our little sin is, somehow, worse than the brutal execution of Jesus?

---

[7] Matthew 12:31 (NAB).

[8] Luke 23:34a (NAB).

If God can forgive the murderers of His Son, God can certainly forgive you. Does it matter to God that we have sinned? Yes. Is that sin the end of God's plans, God's mercy, God's love? No.

DIABOLICAL MECHANISMS

Some of the most sinister weapons of the devil are invisible to the unreflective mind. We often need to work together, with the great minds and saints of the centuries, to discover these diabolic mechanisms. I would like to briefly describe one such mechanism here. It is the basis of Rene Girard's Theology.[9] It is the **Scapegoat Mechanism.**

Sometimes we participate in certain common mentalities that we do not realize are the old mechanisms of our Ancient Foe: we find someone to blame for whatever is going wrong. Then, we gather with others who agree with us, and we complain about that person as the "culprit." Along the way, we come up with a plan to deal with the culprit in a way that seems justified and feels like a solution to the problem. Then we act on this plan by belittling, isolating, shunning, exiling, hurting, or even killing the culprit.

For example, a football team was going to a game out of town. They wanted to stop for dinner and were throwing around some suggestions. One of the boys, Alec, suggested a specific restaurant that was his favorite. Though some had opposing suggestions, for the sake of making a decision, they all agreed to go to Alec's restau-

---

[9] René Girard, *The Scapegoat*, trans. Yvonne Freccero (Baltimore, MD: Johns Hopkins University Press, 1986).

rant. Unfortunately, they all got food poisoning and ended up having to cancel the game. They spent the night at the hospital recovering.

That whole week, the members of the team were angry they had to forfeit the game. As they complained about it, the conversation began to focus on Alec. They decided it was his fault because he chose the restaurant. If they had gone to any of the other suggested places, they would not have gotten sick. As they worked themselves into a frenzy, they decided to rough up Alec and make sure he was benched for the next game. No one sat with or spoke to him the whole week. Afterward, the other teammates felt pretty justified and satisfied with what they had done. It was a bonding moment for everyone except Alec.

This scenario frequently plays out in corporate America, politics, friendships, families, schools, and even parishes. Wherever there are people, we will find this Scapegoat Mechanism at play.

Though we are not conscious of it, we have inadvertently fallen into the devil's trap. Amazingly, it seems to work. The mob feels closer as a result. The culprit does not do it again. The bad feelings from the predicament go away. Yet, it is all just an illusion. Soon, there will be another problem, and they will have to find another culprit. Then another. Then another. Though it seems like it leads to peace and a remedy to the problems, scapegoating only results in victimizing each other and temporarily distracting everyone from the real issue. The "culprit" is really an arbitrary victim who takes the brunt of other people's pain and frustrations. Alec had nothing to do with the food poisoning, but that becomes irrelevant once the Scapegoat Mechanism begins to work on the mob-mentality.

We see this same mechanism at work in Jesus' day. The Pharisees brought a woman caught in the act of adultery to Jesus.[10] They suggested stoning her according to the Law of Moses and asked Jesus' opinion on the matter. They were testing Jesus to see if He would be on their side, the side of righteousness, or continue with His "love of sinners." In response, Jesus said, "He who has no sin, throw the first stone." It was a brilliant way to disarm the Scapegoat Mechanism. Today, we do the same thing the Pharisees did. We call this woman the "culprit" and blame her for our problems. We may not be able to solve all the issues with Israel, but this problem has a "solution." We feel justified because of her sins, but the truth is that we are all sinners. If we are constantly looking for some sinner to blame for the problems of the world, we put ourselves in danger. Tomorrow, it could be any of us. The Gospel says that, one by one, the crowd walked away. Instead of finding unity in the mob that wanted to kill this woman together, they are left individually contemplating how they, too, need to stop sinning and stop looking for someone to blame for the problems of the world.

When I was younger, I thought the world was filled with basically good people. As I experienced the world outside of the protective bubble of my parents and community, I came to realize that there are wicked people out there; some more dastardly than I could have imagined. I comforted myself with the fantasy of dividing the world into the good and the bad. I imagined a fortified city with impenetrable walls keeping us safe from the corrupt. We could round up, eliminate, or cast out the wicked and make it a better world. The

---

[10] John 8:4-11 (NAB).

more I experienced the work of a priest, the more I realized that the world is not so clearly delineated between the good and the bad. Jesus told us that the weeds and the wheat would have to coexist in this world.[11] The separation happens afterward. Besides, each of us is both good and bad at different times and in different circumstances. How bad is too bad?

As I experience the **Ministry of Mercy** that is part of the life of a priest, I have come to pity the sinner. The circumstances and poor choices of their lives have misshapen them into the wicked people they have become. Once, I prayed with a gang member who had seen and done terrible things. The fifteen-year-old cried as he told me that he missed his mother and the little boy he used to be. On another occasion, I visited a juvenile delinquency center and heard the witness of one of the teenagers. He told me that his grades, health, and attitude have never been better since he was arrested. He felt accomplished, loved, and supported. He was terrified at the idea of leaving the center. "The same group of guys that I used to hang out with is waiting for me at the corner. It is just a matter of time before they turn me back into the failure I used to be." I find my heart desires the repentance, conversion, and salvation of sinners. I want them to be the people God knows they can become. I love the sinner, more than ever, as I realize the meaning of God's plan. God saves me, though I do not deserve it. Through God's grace, even I can become a saint. What about these least of God's people? Am I not called to love them as God loves me?[12]

---

[11] Matthew 13:24-30 (NAB).

[12] See Matthew 25:40 (NAB).

The "wicked" have begun to lose hope, but I have not. I am not being naïve. I do not trust a person who has sinned many times. I do not think they should trust themselves. Their moral fortitude is considerably weakened because of their sinful past. Nonetheless, I do not discount them from being worthy of love and the hope of redemption. St. Thérèse of Lisieux at age sixteen, before she entered into the cloistered Carmelite convent, prayed fervently for a wicked man who was condemned to death.[13] Though he had been vehemently against allowing a priest to visit with him, the night before his execution, he repented and kissed the wounds of Jesus on the crucifix of the priest was wearing. St. Thérèse considered this the first, but not the last, of the souls she intended to help through her ardent prayers. The last words of St. Maria Goretti were forgiveness for her murderer.[14] Seven years later, the murderer had a vision of Maria forgiving him again. Though he had been completely unrepentant and opposed to holiness up until this point, the man had a complete conversion, became a model prisoner, then a Capuchin, and is now being considered for beatification.

The Tempter has many such weapons in his arsenal, like the Scapegoat Mechanism. A good spiritual director will help you see through some of the blindness of the "mob mentality" to the true nature of the sin. Instead of finding culprits, we are called to love our enemies, do good to those who harm us, and forgive the sinner.[15] A

---

[13] Therese of Lisieux, *Story of a Soul*, 99-100.

[14] Jeffrey Kirby, *The Life and Witness of Saint Maria Goretti: Our Little Saint of the Beatitudes* (Charlotte, NC: TAN Books, 2015), 35-38.

[15] Matthew 5:44 (NAB).

sure way of knowing we are getting wrapped up in a diabolic mechanism is when we claim, "I know what I am supposed to do, but this case is different." The Tempter is clever. We must make our defense by following the way of the Lord, even if it seems too simple.

Chapter 6

Progressing in Spiritual Maturity

It is my understanding that every person is at a different stage of spiritual development. It is counterproductive to assume that we can use same approach to help all people grow in their relationship with God. Instead, parishes should use a variety of ministries and methods to reach people at whatever stage they may be. The hope is that the parish community can help each person take one step forward in his personal journey of faith.

I have categorized six stages of the **Journey of Faith** of a typical person. People often skip steps, but I find it useful to backtrack and complete earlier steps before proceeding onward. There should be no sense that people in one step are better than people in another. God loves us right where we are. The goal is to help each person take just one step forward in this journey of becoming a more authentic disciple of the Lord. It takes patience and confidence that, in their own time and at their own speed, people will continue on the path. We merely walk with them on the journey. This is what Pope Francis calls, "**Accompaniment**."[1]

The progression through the six stages of the Journey of Faith has become my understanding of diocesan parish spirituality. It is the backbone of my Parish Pastoral Plan and my basic approach to all that I do in the parish.

The first stage of the Journey of Faith is the traditional **Evangelization Stage**. People in this stage go from being apathetic about faith, to being interested, and eventually to believing that there is some truth in the faith. There is no commitment at this level. It is almost purely an intellectual or affective experience. Those in this stage are not in church on Sundays. To reach this group, which represents most Americans, we must find innovative ways of presenting faith to them. Advertising techniques and personal relationships are the most effective forms of evangelization at this stage. Think about billboards, websites, television commercials and programs, and conversations with friends.

The second stage of the Journey of Faith is the **Spiritual Awakening Stage**. At this stage, a person has some sort of mystical, spir-

---

[1] Francis, "Evangelii Gaudium": Apostolic Exhortation on the Proclamation of the Gospel in Today's World, November 24, 2013, https://www.vatican.va/content/francesco/en/apost_exhortations/documents/papa-francesco_esortazione-ap_20131124_evangelii-gaudium.html#Personal_accompaniment_in_processes_of_growth, paragraphs 169-173.

itual encounter with the Lord. It is usually both exciting and disorienting. Hopefully, the person moves toward trusting Christ, whom he encountered. The best place to evoke this stage is through a retreat setting. This helps move Christ from a thought experience or a historical figure to a living, active Person in our lives.

The third stage of the Journey of Faith is the **Church Community Stage**. This is the point at which people begin to look to the Church for answers to their new questions. They can pursue these answers either by reading or by talking to members of the parish. As their relationship and comfort with the Church grow, we hope that people in this group begin to attend a parish regularly. They learn, not only how to pray with the crowd, but how to begin to develop a personal prayer life. I find that many "cradle Catholics" are in this category, but they have not had the chance to develop a personal relationship with Christ through an encounter with the Risen Lord. It is best to go back and complete the second stage before continuing to the next stage. Sometimes this means that we stay at this stage until God gifts us with the graces to move forward. Wait for the Lord.

The fourth stage of the Journey of Faith is the **Conversion Stage**. People at this stage have an awakening that there is a moral law beyond the universal norms. It is not enough that we have never killed anyone. We must love everyone. This moral awakening leads to a conversion when people want to change their lives to become the disciples Christ deserves. Then, people must examine all other aspects of their lives to see if anything needs to change based on their conversion. I call this "metanoia of life." These people may discover that, if they are to take seriously their conversion, it is no longer acceptable, for example, to work for a porn shop. The ripple effect of the conversion must reach all areas of their lives. They must completely reject sin. I find that retreats, counsel from a good advisor, and, of course, the Sacrament of Reconciliation, are the best ways to help people through this stage.

The fifth stage of the Journey of Faith is the **Discipleship Stage**. At this stage, people commit to use their time, talent, and treasure to serve the Lord. They are willing to devote time and energy toward a ministry of interest. Eventually, they learn how to let the Holy Spirit direct them toward a specific ministry. This occurs when they are not merely getting involved in the things they enjoy doing, but they are actively asking God what He desires them to do. I have a special retreat designed for this purpose, called the Discipleship Retreat. After the retreat, I meet with all the participants individually to pray with them about their discernment of the ministry God is calling them to do.

The last stage of the Journey of Faith is the **Missionary Stage**. At this stage, people are guided by the Holy Spirit to consider the Catholic Vision, the Prophetic Role, and the Call to Leadership. The Catholic Vision is when we become aware of the activity of the Church and the needs of the people outside of our regular circle of interest and acquaintances. It is when we begin to wonder about the people in El Salvador, Ghana, Sri Lanka, the Cleveland Housing Projects, etc. The Prophetic Role is when we realize that God's work and our mission are actually reshaping the world. We see our efforts in the fullness of time and in the big picture. We recognize that we are collaborating with God in the redemption of the world! Finally, the

Call to Leadership is when we are prompted by the Holy Spirit to coordinate with others, within the context of the Church, toward a common mission. It requires a respect for the spiritual gifts and human abilities of others and a vision of how we can collaborate as members of the Mystical Body of Christ.

Using the six stages of the Journey of Faith, I am able to recognize how each ministry can be used to further people in their spiritual development. I simply identify the stage at which a person currently is and connect him to the ministry that best suits the spiritual needs of that stage. It is less about following the whims of our desires and more about systematically leading people toward a deeper relationship with Christ.

The Journey of Faith also helps ministries and parish groups set goals and stay focused on those goals. It highlights that they are an important part of the entire parish mission. Finally, it allows parish groups to appreciate other ministries and support each other in their interconnected goals. No single ministry or parish group has to do everything, nor is there any need to compete for participants, which is often the case. When appropriate, they may refer members to other groups.

VIRTUE BUILDING

We are all sinners. That is why we need a Savior. Yet, just because we have a Savior does not mean we are permitted to continue sinning. It is another sin piled onto our mountain of sins to **Presume God's Mercy**. We must at least make a sincere and diligent effort to stop sinning and to begin living holy lives.

All sin begins with **Temptation**. Temptation is an attraction to act contrary to right reason and the commandments of God.[2] In the movies, it is visualized as an angel on one shoulder and a devil on the other. In reality, though, temptation occurs as a way of thinking about and evaluating options and the desired outcomes of those options. Some sins are relatively inconsequential. Some sins are committed out of ignorance, that is, the person did not realize it was a sin. Sometimes people are pressured to sin by forces beyond their control. These sins are called **Venial Sins**.[3] A **Mortal Sin** is a serious matter (significant consequences), committed while the person fully understands the options available and fully understands that this option offends God, and committed freely.[4]

Venial Sins, while offensive to God who deserves all our love, do not put our eternal salvation in jeopardy. Mortal sins, on the other hand, break our friendship with God and must be healed in order to reestablish a good relationship. For example, telling a friend that he has a big nose offends him, but he is still your friend (venial). Throwing a friend out of a moving vehicle with the intent of hurting him destroys your friendship (mortal). Whenever we are aware of venial sins, against God or others, it is appropriate to seek pardon. This is a way of loving more perfectly and respecting the glory of God more fully. When we commit a mortal sin, it is important to take that sin to the Sacrament of Reconciliation as soon as possible. We should not receive Holy Communion until the mortal sin is properly forgiven. I do not suggest waiting long before going to the Sacrament.

---

[2] *Catechism of the Catholic Church*, glossary, "Temptation."

[3] *Catechism of the Catholic Church*, paragraph 1862.

[4] *Catechism of the Catholic Church*, paragraph 1857.

We all need those graces. By disrupting our relationship with Christ, mortal sin limits the graces we are able to receive. If we want to live in God's grace, we should strive to be holy and cleansed of our known serious offenses. God will do much more through us when we are "in His good graces."

Many people prefer not to confess their sins to a priest. They hope that it suffices simply to be sorry for their sins and, maybe, to do a personal prayer of repentance. To be clear, I do not limit God's mercy to the confessional. God is certainly free to forgive in any way He wishes. I earnestly hope that all people are forgiven, even those who do not go to the Sacrament. Yet, Christ gave us the Sacrament to forgive our sins for a reason. I am not so arrogant as to argue with God that forgiveness should have been given to us in another way. Christ said to the Apostles, "Whose sins you forgive are forgiven them, and whose sins you retrained are retained."[5] This ministry continues today through the priesthood.

I think, from a very human perspective, the humbling act of admitting our sins to another person demonstrates and makes more effective our true sorrow for our sins. In Alcoholics Anonymous, the fifth step is, "Admit… to God, to ourselves, and to another human being the exact nature of our wrongs."[6] Seeing how effective Alcoholics Anonymous has been, there must be something about the ritual of telling another person our sins that is healing and freeing for us. In addition, I believe there is a value to hearing the words, "I absolve you from your sins." As we yell at the sky or in our minds that

---

[5] John 20:23 (NAB).

[6] "The Twelve Steps."

we are sorry for our sins, we get no response. In the Sacrament of Reconciliation, God sends His priest with this message: "I forgive you."

Each of us struggles with our own temptations, as if the Tempter had designed specific traps for every person. Temptation is a reality that all humanity faces, including Christ.[7] Because of our specific opportunities, influences, and past mistakes, some temptations tend to be stronger than others, depending on the individual. We do not often speak about our temptations because we fear being judged and our past sins being exposed. We are ashamed. Yet, if we never confront our temptations and always keep spiritual conversations and practice superficial, we can never overcome our personal temptations. We must have the courage to mature spiritually.

Spiritual direction is a safe place to expose those temptations without feeling judged. Once we name a temptation, we can take responsibility for it. We can mentally separate it from ourselves and make it less connected with our identity. Then we can formulate a strategy to protect ourselves from that Temptation until it loses its influence on us. We are not our sins. We are not our temptations. We will not lose ourselves if we remove sin and temptation from our lives.

This method of spiritual growth I call **virtue building**. First, we name the sin that tempts us. Then, we name the opposite virtue that we are hoping to gain. The goal is to develop this holy behavior and attitude to the point that it becomes an effortless, even automatic, response in our daily lives. This virtue cannot exist simultaneously

---

[7] Mark 1:13 (NAB).

with sinful behavior or attitudes. Instead of feeling inclined to slide toward the sin (vice), we are inclined toward holiness (virtue). Vice and virtue are like weights on a scale, where one will always outweigh the other, so we need to ensure our virtue is stronger than our vice.

Next, we have to be creative to find spiritual practices that will help us to grow those specific virtues that are underdeveloped. I call these spiritual practices that are designed to develop virtue "**Penances**". Since we have spent so much of our lives developing the vices, it may take time and considerable energy to develop their opposites, the virtues. Do not be discouraged. Others have been successful; we can succeed too.

In naming our vices, we can use various lists. *The Seven Deadly Sins* are a good start. For each of the seven sins, I will attempt to name the opposite virtues. Then, I will make suggestions on penances that may be helpful, as well as comment on penances that do not help develop those virtues. My list will not be exhaustive nor will my techniques for developing virtue be universally applicable, but they may inspire others to find creative solutions as well.

PRIDE

The sin of **Pride** is an inaccurate estimation of one's own importance and proper role in a relationship. This includes being self-centered, selfish, inconsiderate, judgmental, considering yourself superior (or inferior) to others, vanity, false humility, or looking for honors, adoration, attention, or unearned respect. The opposite virtue is **Humility**, which includes being accepting of yourself as you are without the need for recognition and placing the needs of others before your own. To grow in humility, an appropriate penance might be to spend time actively listening to someone else without drawing the focus of the conversation back to yourself. Or meet with your family and let them remind you of the funny mistakes you made as a child. Be willing to laugh at yourself.

Another suggestion to overcome pride is to make a mental list of your strengths and weaknesses. See that list as a call from God to enter into community. Think of someone who could benefit from one of your specific gifts. Now think of someone who could help you with one of your shortcomings. Use your gifts to help each other.

A remedy for pride could be to anonymously perform a menial, service-oriented task that requires none of your stronger gifts. Remember the example of *The Little Way* of St. Thérèse.[8] The great deeds we do are not that great to God. Therefore, the little acts of kindness and penance are just as valuable to God as any of the great achievements of the saints. Be willing to be little.

Another suggested penance is to recall a time that someone misjudged you. Instead of getting upset, realize that you have probably done the same thing to others. Spend some time recognizing how quickly you judged a specific person without really knowing his situation.

Finally, be especially obedient to someone else's decision, even if you think you have a better solution, so long as the decision is not wicked. For example, choose to take the route to the store that your spouse suggests without arguing about your superior, faster route.

---

[8] Therese of Lisieux, *Story of a Soul.*

ENVY

Envy is the sin of desiring the blessings of others or wishing that others did not have such blessings. The opposite virtue is **Gratitude**. To grow in gratitude, make a list of the things that you consider your greatest blessings. Or consider the difficulties people face in an impoverished country. Or write a personal prayer of thanksgiving to the best of your ability. Or contemplate the blessings of the things you do *not* have, including sickness and troubles in life, as well as temptations you would probably not have handled well, such as fame or money. I often thank God that I am not too ugly and not too good-looking. Either way would have been a problem for me. Finally, design a prayer of petition listing the blessings you want your children to have. Try to be sincere. You may include why you want them to have those blessings.

I often hear among Catholics, even the clergy, a sense of envy concerning the large numbers of participants and collections at Evangelical **Megachurches.** Do not let envy into your heart. First of all, the population of any given megachurch is taken from a huge territory. How many Catholic parishes would that include? Secondly, most of the megachurches are very dependent on a charismatic personality. They do not last after one generation. Thirdly, megachurches may be awakening the faith of people who are either dormant in their faith life or spiritually starving. It may be God's plan to work through these churches for now. At some later date, perhaps the people or their children will be ready to return to the Catholic parishes. Perhaps the Catholic parishes would work harder for converts if they did not operate as if they have a virtual monopoly on the church options.

As a seminarian, I was assigned to a parish that had virtually no homes in its territorial boundaries, yet it consistently had a large number of people wanting to become Catholic at the Easter Vigil. The surrounding Evangelical churches were excellent at evangelizing and inviting people to Christianity. They made the Faith exciting and accessible. As their emotions calmed down and there was a desire for some of the more steeped Traditions and teachings, people found their way over to the Catholic parish. Perhaps this is God's plan. Hopefully, we will all become better at bringing Christ to the people and working, each with our own gifts, to bring souls to Christ.

GLUTTONY

Gluttony is a disordered desire for food or drink (or other goods) beyond its natural purpose to sustain the health of the body or mind. The opposite virtue to gluttony is **temperance**, also known as **moderation**. Fasting is a favorite penance to combat gluttony, but it often leads to overeating afterward. It is the recognition that, though my body has certain desires, I am willing to sacrifice those desires for a greater desire: Grace. Fasting may not be the best penance since it focuses on the food. For those who struggle with eating disorders, this can become problematic. Other penances might be to enjoy things more slowly, make a sincere prayer of thanksgiving before enjoying whatever it is, remember those who go without the abundance you have, or simplify your meals with less flavor so as to decrease your appetite.

LUST

Lust is disordered desire for an inordinate enjoyment of sexual pleasure; when sexual pleasure is sought for itself, apart from the unitive and procreative function.[9] Lust includes pornography, masturbation, fornication, adultery, sexual fantasies, inappropriate scenes in movies or books designed to sexually stimulate, separating sex from authentic love, sexual abuse, a lack of discretion in conversations about sex, or fostering romantic desire for someone other than your spouse or potential spouse. The opposite virtue is **Chastity**. Penances can help reorient the mind to proper respect for other people as being more than sexual entertainment. One such penance is to imagine the people in question are your relatives. How would you want someone to see them? You would want them to be appreciated for their beauty, but not become objects. In your mind, imagine someone looking at your relatives the way you look at other people.

Another suggestion is to study St. John Paul II's *Theology of the Body*.[10] An additional tool is to work with a spiritual director to discover the roots of some of your thinking about sex that may be twisted. Were there movies or experiences from your youth that

---

[9] *Catechism of the Catholic Church*, paragraph 235.

[10] Christopher West, *Theology of the Body Explained: A Commentary on John Paul II's "Man and Woman He Created Them"* (Boston, MA: Pauline Books & Media, 2007).

gave you a misguided impression about sex? When you identify a moment, ask God to heal the wound and restore chastity.

Finally, so long as it does not lead you into further temptation, it may be helpful to be a support for others who have been abused sexually. This may be simply reading testimonies or going to a speech about someone's ordeal and the healing process. As you realize the harm that is caused, you will be fortified not to be the cause of someone else's misery.

It should be noted that we must distinguish between Voluntary and Involuntary Thoughts with regard to sexual thoughts. **Involuntary Thoughts** pop into our minds without our freely choosing. If I say, "Don't think of an elephant." Too late, you just did. Sexual thoughts occasionally pop into our minds, especially in a world obsessed with sex. These Involuntary Thoughts are not sins. Just recognize them for what they are, and let them go. **Voluntary Thoughts**, on the other hand, are fantasies, schemes, or intentionally dwelling on immoral subject matter. Having planned to rob a bank and then losing the guts to go through with it is still a sin. In much the same way, voluntary sexual thoughts are included in the category of Lust and should be confessed and renounced. They change the way we think and the way we treat others, even if just subconsciously.

I also want to note a spiritual image, called "**Salt Water**," that I use to describe the ill-effects of pornography. Pornography is like being in a boat in the middle of the ocean without supplies. As you get thirsty, you may be tempted to drink the saltwater. Don't do it! It will not take away your thirst. It will make your thirst worse and worse until you are very sick. Though you may be very thirsty, you are far better off waiting for the proper port so that you can drink freshwater. Pornography will never satisfy your lust. It will just make you more 'thirsty,' and, eventually, make you sick.

WRATH

The sin of **wrath** is the willingness to justify not desiring the good of the other based on a self-authorized sense of justice. This includes revenge, resentment, passive-aggressive behavior, violence, verbal abuse, unforgiveness, slander, and wishing harm on someone. It should be noted that "anger" is a feeling. Wrath is the weaponizing of anger. Some people think anger and wrath are the same thing. However, a person may be angry at an injustice, but does not then justify willing the bad upon a culprit because they are not the proper authority. The opposite of wrath is the virtue of **charity**. It may be necessary to make amends for past outbursts or offenses. It may be necessary to forgive someone or seek their forgiveness. A spiritual director can help you name the hurt that was inflicted. Lasting wounds usually include some lie about ourselves or a truth that we do not want to admit. Naming the wound may help the healing process.

Jesus says that we are supposed to "love our enemies."[11] A penance could be to pray about a creative and practical way you can fulfill the Lord's command with that person who has been the victim of your anger. You know who it is.

---

[11] Matthew 5:44 (NAB).

Another penance is to work with a spiritual director to find solutions to the problem, rather than spreading discontent and trying to justify your anger. Another penance might be to recognize times in the past when you have offended others. Maybe they forgave you, or maybe not. The humble realization that we make the same mistake that others have made against us should lower our sense of outrage. We all make mistakes and could use some mercy.

Inevitably, we encounter **Conflict** with people around us. Most conflicts are rooted in an injustice that needs healing, a confusion that needs clarification, or opposing paradigms of thinking and methods of reaching goals. In resolving conflicts, it is important to remember the goal of the encounter. Are you trying to bring healing, clarification, or agreeing to disagree about perspectives and methodologies? Has this person insulted you and you are looking to restore the relationship? Is there a disconnection between what has been communicated or understood and what was intended? Is there a fundamental difference in the way you understand the world based on your different life experiences? Are there two ways to reach the same goal?

There is a tendency to become **Defensive** when dealing with conflict. This often occurs when a person is too closely associated with the opinion or issue at hand. If someone else rejects his opinion, it may feel like a personal rejection. This can cause him to attempt to find any support for his position, regardless of the illogic or inconsistencies.

Defensiveness may also cause a counter-reaction of attacking the dignity of the other person. Disregarding the issue of the conflict, a person may attempt to belittle the other person and his position. "What does he know, anyway? He's just a (fill in the blank)."

Defensiveness may cause a person to isolate or intimidate the other person in order to silence the conflict and dominate the decision. This is a sin against charity.

Defensiveness can also lead people to avoid the issue, despite having inner conflict. This can cause people to have resentments that affect relationships and decisions regarding the other person. It may manifest in "talking behind someone's back," slander, or an exaggeration of the personal flaws or flawed thinking of the other person to sway the judgment of other people toward your cause or away from the other person. It is an attempt to remove the other person's support in order to belittle him and silence his opinion. Again, this is a sin against charity and shows a lack of respect for the other person.

Finally, defensiveness can cause a temptation to express to other people a sense of being wounded, especially when you suspect that you are wrong with regard to the issue. This is an attempt to seek compassion and support for yourself as the "victim." It is a way of turning people against the other person, changing the topic of the issue to a personal attack, and judging the worthiness and legitimacy of the other person's right to express his opinions and disagree with you.

In the Scriptures, Jesus gives a teaching about resolving conflict that is much more charitable than anger and defensiveness. "If your brother sins against you, go and tell him his fault between you and him alone. If he listens to you, you have won over your brother. If he does not listen, take one or two others along with you, so that 'every fact may be established on the testimony of two or three witnesses.' If he refuses to listen to them, tell the church. If he refuses to listen even to the church, then treat him as you would a Gentile or a tax collector."[12] Jesus is giving four progressive steps: Talk directly to the person, involve a few mutual friends who can be objective, look to a higher authority to resolve the issue, or charitably avoid each other so as not to make the matter worse.

If I may be so bold as to add to Jesus' steps a preliminary step: Put on the right mindset before speaking to the individual. Often, we need to calm our emotions (and the other person's) to see the issue more clearly, avoid being defensive, and be prepared for the outcome of the discussion. The principle of Holy Indifference should be applied here. Clearly, you think you are right about an issue. If additional information proves that you are mistaken, are you prepared to change your position and humbly accept the reasoning of the other person? If you are not willing to change, then your desire is merely to "win" or to dominate. Seek healing and Truth, and try to work together. Sufficiently separate your identity from the issue so as to be ready to accept any decision that results from the encounter.

Some things are worth fighting about. Some things are not. **Pick Your Battles** according to the greater goals of the community, relationship, and mission of the Church. Not everyone needs to agree with you for your community to function well. A diversity of paradigms of thinking is healthy for a community because it allows for creative problem solving. A scraped knee will heal without any long-

---

[12] Matthew 18:15-17 (NAB).

lasting consequences. Not every conflict result in lasting wounds, either. Eventually, some problems will go away on their own. The prudence we ask of God is to know when the situation calls for a more significant response or patience to let the problem pass. Some conflicts will not heal without attention. Some people are more open to resolving issues than other people. Know your audience and estimate the emotional energy required for the conflict to be sufficiently resolved. Is it worth it? Sometimes it is. Sometimes issues are more significant to you than they are to others or vice-versa.

Love is the only reason for entering into an attempt to resolve conflict. It is not about justifying yourself or dominating others. If you are corrected, rejoice. The other person has made you better equipped to make good decisions. If you correct another person, let it be only to help the other person to be even better. Avoid bringing disharmony into the community.

One day, when I was dealing with social pressures, failure, public embarrassment, and insecurity, my dad had a little talk with me. He said, "Michael, do you know what most people think of you? They don't." It is true. Most people are not thinking about me at all, or if they are, it is only very minimally. On one level, I suppose that makes us feel less significant. In our minds, are we not always thinking about ourselves? Our wants? Our fears? Our goals? Our perspectives? How other people relate to us? Most people are thinking about themselves, too. They are not thinking about us. On the other hand, this was very comforting advice from my dad. We often take ourselves too seriously, losing the perspective that the world does not depend on us. We do not have to get everything right, have the perfect words, or be having the perfect day, every day. It all keeps moving with or without us.

Breaking me out of my panic-inducing trance, my father helped me to recognize that I am part of a greater community. People are not all thinking exactly what I assume they are. We are all on different, though related, journeys with our own perspectives, needs, and fears. This provides a variety of options and opportunities to relate to each other and be helpful to one another. Besides, we cause most of our own mental suffering by placing too much responsibility and importance on ourselves.

Knowing this about myself gave me great peace. It also made me realize the anxieties and difficulties other people must be enduring. I came to understand why Christ was so lenient toward the repentant sinners and so harsh with the judgmental righteous. "They tie up heavy burdens hard to carry and lay them on people's shoulders, but they will not lift a finger to move them."[13] I had fallen into a pattern of self-inflicted suffering of putting the burden of the world on my shoulders. Remember, we have a Savior, and it is not you.

I began to see the value in the spirituality of being **Other-Centered**. Christ's teachings and the application of those teachings by the saints of the Church continually instruct us to be less concerned with ourselves and more concerned about our neighbor. This has two practical meanings. First, we find our fulfillment in being members of a community and offering assistance to others. True happiness and contentment are not found somewhere "out there." They

---

[13] Matthew 23:4 (NAB).

will come to us when we begin to live the right way. I suppose that is why we see people in poor nations being joyful and fulfilled, despite not having all the things we thought no one could live without. Secondly, we do not have to do everything ourselves. As members of a community, we can ask for help and work together toward the greater goal of the Divine Plan.

Tolerance, in itself, is not strictly a virtue. It may be used as a way of avoiding conflict or accepting one's responsibility to fraternally correct. However, when exercised with prudence, a person can be a virtuous. Instead of wrath, a person may choose to either patiently and humbly overlook the flaw or mistake in another person or they can choose to enter into a conflict to correct the flaw or mistake of the other. The proper response depends on the right relationship of the parties, the seriousness of the issue, the context (in front of others or in private with a trusted friend), and the reasonable expectation of a positive outcome. In other words, we need prudence on when to be tolerant. A penance to build tolerance might be a mental exercise to recognize that many people tolerate you. We all are probably annoying to some people sometimes. Yet, people tolerate your droning on about personal issues, not getting tasks done, or telling the same story repeatedly. Their tolerance is a way of loving and respecting you. Recognizing this humbling fact may change the way we handle others who annoy us.

Even those who are unjustly critical of us may be, intentionally or unintentionally, helping us to become better. As St. Paul tells the Corinthians in his Second Letter, "If I have saddened you by my letter (of criticism) I have no regrets… because your sadness led to repentance ... leading to salvation."[14] Even if the criticism was unfounded, it still may evoke God's mercy. Remember King David tolerating Shimei, who was cursing and throwing rocks at him. David prayed that, if he would humbly tolerate the insults, perhaps God would show him mercy.[15] When we humbly tolerate insults without lashing back, we have, essentially, "turned the other cheek."[16]

GREED

The sin of **Greed** is the disordered accumulation of material goods at the expense of appropriate immediate needs. This includes a disordered desire for more things or time, a disordered fear of losing what you have, or a disordered unwillingness to share your resources. This may include taking rewards, payments, and benefits that are not earned or appropriate through stealing, intimidation, or fraud. It may also include reckless gambling. The opposite virtue is **Generosity**, also known as **Stewardship**. I do not recommend merely donating to charity. This activity would reinforce the central place of money as a solution and the lack of resources as a problem. Some helpful penances may include spending a day relaxing without spending money. You can go to the beach, eat from a garden, exercise, or visit friends. Another penance is to prayerfully prepare a budget that gives authority over some part of the budget to other family members. For example, if there is charitable giving including

[14] 2 Corinthians 7:8-9 (NAB).

[15] 2 Samuel 16:5-14 (NAB).

[16] Matthew 5:39 (NAB).

in the family budget, let your spouse and children choose the beneficiaries and the percentages within that budget. Allowing your resources to be dictated by prayer and those you love helps to remove the controlling aspect of greed.

Another way in which we can be freed from the temptation to greed is to identify and renounce our **Attachments**. Clearly, we need certain things to be healthy: nourishment, a range of temperatures, friendships, medicine, protection from the elements and dangers, etc. However, there is a great deal in our lives that is not necessary. For example, too much rest, food, comfort, entertainment, distraction, control over situations, attention from certain people, caffeine, etc. I remember telling the children in my U.S. parish about my experiences as a missionary. They were horrified at the idea of being in a location with no electricity because it meant they would have to go without cell phones, video games, or television. Even some adults cannot fathom living without alcohol, sports, or the comforts of their homes. Having an unhealthy dependence on things or people can be a contributing factor to greed since it fills us with the fear of losing those unnecessary, but seemingly important, parts of our lives. A penance may be to identify one of those attachments and work on being free from that excessive reliance. Instead, work on relying solely on God. This, of course, matches our Lenten sacrifices. Also, this practice can help fortify our willpower for the occasions when we have to sacrifice our desires for the sake of God's Kingdom.

SLOTH

The sin of **sloth** is preferring a state of rest over activity, in particular when it comes to one's duties. This includes sins of omission in your duties and not being proactive in helping others or initiating projects. The opposite virtue is **diligence**. Possible penances include writing task lists, getting started with a project, cleaning out some part of the house or office, exercising, doing manual labor, or helping out a friend with a project.

For most people, the issue of sloth is a question of inertia. They need to "get the ball moving" and it gains momentum from that point forward. In physics, it is said that an object at rest tends to stay at rest. The same is true for human beings: many of us struggle to begin a project because it would require a change from a state of rest. Once we initiate the task, it seems to be much easier to continue. Get past the first step.

Be aware of the possibility of depression, which is a psychological or chemical state that makes a person unwilling or unable to engage in activity. Depression can be the result of a situation, like grieving the loss of a friend. It can also be a biological reaction to diet or genetics. This would require a professional to diagnosis and address it.

Other virtues to develop include **Patience** (allowing time for people and events to adjust)**, Honesty** (accepting and responding to a reality that does not match the ideal)**, and Reverence** (recognizing and respecting the dignity of each person, ourselves, creation, and

God). To develop patience, I do not recommend sending an impatient person to work with children or the elderly. That runs the risk of victimizing people. Instead, I recommend finding a balance of downtime, work, exercise, and prayer. In prayer time, we can use the Ignatian *Examen*[17] to anticipate stressful situations that usually lead to impatience. We can then prepare themselves spiritually and mentally to handle the situation. In retrospect, we can focus their energies less on justifying their impatience and more on prayerfully finding other options to handle the situation better in the future. We may ask, "What would Saint (fill in the blank) do in my situation?"

To develop honesty, utilize the **Three-Second Rule**. When people who struggle with honesty are feeling pressured, their first reaction is to fabricate a story according to what they think will give their desired result. They may be seeking attention or admiration. That is pride. They may be avoiding responsibility. That is sloth. They may be simply repeating a lie that they forgot was not true. The Three-Second Rule states that, when a person feels pressured before speaking, he must mentally count to three before responding. This helps lower the impulsive reaction to fabricate a story and helps him return to the truth. Remember not to tell a half-truth. Tell the whole truth. Even though they may not receive praise and may even face consequences, internally they can throw a little party! They passed the test and are beginning to grow.

---

[17] Ignatius of Loyola, *The Text of the Spiritual Exercises of Saint Ignatius*, 13.

Sometimes people do not realize how serious of a sin lying can be. It is forbidden in the Ten Commandments for a reason. The Gospel we have received is of the utmost importance. It is our duty and our identity to be proclaimers of the Good News. If people cannot trust us in small matters, they will not trust us in big matters, like salvation.[18]

To help people understand the courage and seriousness required to be honest, I invite them to contemplate **Jesus Before Pontius Pilate**. During Jesus' trial, Pilate mocks Him, saying, "What is truth?"[19] Jesus refuses to lie, even when the consequences of telling the truth are torture and death. Pilate gives a clear indication that he will let Jesus go if only He will say what is expected of Him. Though so frightened that He was sweating drops of blood, Jesus must tell the Truth. He is "...the Way, the Truth, and the Life."[20] If He chooses to lie, His life will be spared, but His mission will fail. Now, are you His follower, or are you not?

To develop **Reverence**, you must maintain a regular discipline of prayer, Mass, and Confession. Also, be vigilant about avoiding irreverent themes in movies, jokes, or conversations. I am amazed at how many themes from movies float about in my head as I daydream. I have to be careful not to contaminate my creativity with irreverent junk.

Also, be deliberate about performing ritualistic actions, like kneeling, genuflecting, and blessing yourself. I recommend the frequent practice of blessing people in your life. It can be meaningful

---

[18] See Luke 16:10 (NAB).

[19] John 18:38 (NAB).

[20] John 14:6 (NAB).

to a person to hear a relative give a blessing. It can be a powerful witness to bless a friend or a sibling who is going on a trip. It is remarkably efficacious to bless a person who is stressed about a task he is going to do.

Finally, a good penance might be to go out of your way to show respect to those who are committed to the spiritual life, including priests, religious, pillars in a faith community, and leaders of other churches. The Mexican parishioners at my church often kiss my hand when I greet them. I am always so humbled by their reverence to a priest. It makes me want to be more reverent to other clergy and religious too.

Virtue building is a life-long endeavor. We will have moments of regressing to our less mature selves. We will have times when we are out of balance due to the situation of life. Continually ask for the grace to recognize and develop the virtues. Though we are required to participate with God's work, it is God who provides the virtues. It is best to think of all people as a work-in-progress. Ask the Lord to bless us with the gifts required to fulfill His holy will.

Chapter 7

The Big Picture: The Plan of Salvation

Many people are under the impression that all people go to Heaven. How I hope that is true! As comforting as the thought might be, it is not the Revelation given to us by God.

The Catholic Church teaches that death is not the end of our existence. After we die, we will face the throne of God for judgment, both personally, at the moment of death, and communally, at the end of the ages. We believe that our personal sin and the sin of humanity (Original Sin) have condemned us to be shunned from the presence of God. By dying for our sins, Jesus redeemed us and saved us from eternal punishment. He opened the gates of Heaven for us.

It is only through Christ that any of us has even the possibility to enter into Heaven.

Many people get stuck on the idea that only Catholics, only Christians, only the baptized, or only those who have accepted Jesus as their "personal Lord and Savior," can enter Heaven. The teaching of the Church is that humanity had lost access to Paradise and only Jesus can restore the hope in salvation. The Church chooses to focus on the nature of Christ, as Savior, rather than on sinners as condemned. Heaven cannot be achieved by the efforts of human beings. Heaven is a gift that Christ offers. We, as Christians, respond to God's love, mercy, and generosity with gratitude by living and trusting in the way of the Lord. Our faithful response to God's love is our acceptance of the gift of eternal life. If any of us, believers and nonbelievers alike, ever have a chance to go to Heaven, it is only through Jesus Christ. Though the practice of faith is the way we gratefully respond to the gift Christ offers us, we never put limitations on the mercy and power of the Cross. In addition, our response to God in faith comes from the grace God gives us: grace to believe, to respond, to worship, to use our God-given talents for His glory. Some can do much in response to God, therefore they should do much. Others can only do a little, depending on the grace God gives them. Therefore, it is only God who knows how much is enough of a response to God's love to be considered sufficiently expressing a grateful acceptance of God's gift of salvation. "Lord, I do believe. Help my unbelief" (Mark 9:24).

When my grandfather was dying, he told me that he believed his wife was in Heaven. He wanted to go and see her. He asked me the most important question anyone has ever asked me, "How do I go to Heaven?" After a few moments of fumbling through my Catholic education, I blurted out, "Jesus! Only through Jesus do we have salvation." My grandfather shook his head in agreement. He then said to me, "How do I receive this gift of Jesus?" Again, I panicked for a moment before responding, "Baptism! The usual way that we unite ourselves with Christ and inherit the promise of everlasting life is through Baptism." At 89 years old, my grandfather requested a priest and was baptized.

Though the **Sacrament of Baptism** is the normative way in which we accept the gift of grace, which is the life of Christ, I would never claim that God's mercy is exclusively for the baptized. Certainly, Moses and Elijah are with the Lord, as was revealed at the Transfiguration. Neither one of them was baptized. Many do not know or believe in Jesus. Can they be saved? The Vatican II document *Lumen Gentium*[1] spells out very well our true belief about who can be saved. Heaven is not an exclusive club, but a gift offered to all people. This is called, "**Universal Salvation.**" Yet, we must accept the gift. We must truly desire to be with the Lord.

Some people remember being taught that Baptism is a requirement to go to Heaven. Thinking that the teaching has changed and the concept of Limbo has been abandoned, some people wonder if it matters if we baptize children. Instead of wondering about this, I simplify the situation. Jesus said, "Go, therefore, and make disciples of all nations, baptizing them in the name of the Father, and of the

---

[1] Paul VI, "Lumen Gentium," Dogmatic Constitution on the Church: Lumen Gentium, Chapter 2, November 21, 1964, https://www.vatican.va/archive/hist_councils/ii_vatican_council/documents/vat-ii_const_19641121_lumen-gentium_en.html.

Son, and of the Holy Spirit."[2] So we do. Christ intentionally leaves a bit of mystery in the Sacrament, not desiring to explain all the reasons or means of God's grace. We are called to trust in His ways. Will God be harsh to a child who was not baptized? A better question is how will God treat the parents who made a solemn oath to baptize their children and have directly opposed a Divine command? That is where the concern is, not with the innocent children.

Some Christian denominations do not baptize children and instead wait for them to have sufficient reasoning to choose Christ personally. Though I think there is a need for a personal choice to follow Christ, I still refer to the command of Christ to "Go and baptize the nations." The "nations" does not refer to rivers and mountains, but to the people of the nations. Children are legitimate people, worthy of love and respect, and they are part of God's plan of salvation. The argument in favor of waiting to baptize children seems to revolve more around the distinction between Personal Sin and Original Sin. A baby does not have personal sin because of a lack of reasoning and, therefore, an inability to choose to sin. Some would argue, since a child cannot sin, there is no need for Baptism. Original Sin, however, is the condition that results in being part of humanity, a fallen, sinful creature. Since I firmly believe that all children are part of humanity, and the reference of the "nations" includes the children, I do as Christ commanded. I focus less on the aspect of sin and more on the identity of the child as a legitimate human being worthy of love and of being part of God's plan of salvation.

---

[2] Matthew 28:19 (NAB).

My parents had a miscarriage before I was born. They unofficially named the child "Joseph." I look forward to seeing Joseph when I die. I have often thought about him. He is, technically, my older brother, but I think of him as a baby brother since he never had the chance to grow old. Yet, he is still my brother. My parents loved him and still love him. I love him. God loves him. In the sadness of death, there is the hope of being reunited with our loved ones. Babies are just as much a part of our human family as any of us.

It is important that our rituals, especially in the Sacraments, authentically convey what they signify. In other words, we want to use the symbolism of the ritual to reveal the invisible reality we believe. We have all met people who say one thing, but their actions tell another story. The man who abuses his girlfriend while telling her he loves her. The crook who talks about wanting to be good while making no effort to become better. The devout person who prays and preaches while stepping over homeless people complaining that they are a nuisance. In St. Paul's letter to the Galatians, he warns us that "**God Will Not Be Mocked.**"[3] We cannot claim that we want to be with Christ for all eternity while our actions say the opposite.

In the Gospel according to St. Matthew, Jesus gives a warning in the form of a parable. He tells about people who took care of the poor, the hungry, the outcasts, the prisoners, and the sick. He explains, "What you did for the least of My people, you did for Me."[4] Then Christ offers them the reward of eternal life. Those who did

---

[3] Galatians 6:7 (NAB).

[4] Matthew 25:40 (NAB).

not care for the poor, the hungry, the outcast, the prisoners, and the sick, despite having claimed to be servants of the Lord, are sent off to eternal punishment. Additionally, in the Gospel according to St. Luke, Jesus gives the parable of the rich man who ignores the needs of a beggar in the street.[5] After they both die, the beggar is with Abraham enjoying comfort and consolation. The rich man, even though he was part of the Chosen People, is suffering fire and thirst because he did not care for those in need. Furthermore, in the Gospel according to St. Mark, Jesus teaches, "If your eye causes you to sin, pluck it out. Better for you to enter the Kingdom of God with one eye than with two eyes be thrown into Gehenna."[6]

Why is Jesus telling His disciples about eternal reward and eternal punishment? Are there really people who go to **Hell**? Though we do not like to think about it, it would seem that Hell is a very real place where a person may go. Even the children at the Marian apparition of Fatima were given the vision of souls in Hell.[7] If we are cautious of the risk of becoming scrupulous, it may be a fruitful spiritual exercise to contemplate what it means to be saved from hell. Do we realize how truly blessed we are to have a Savior? I dare say we will never fully grasp the extent of this gift, which is beyond understanding!

According to Jesus, the determining factor for salvation is the way we live. We either live according to the teachings of Christ, or

---

[5] Luke 16:19-34 (NAB).

[6] Mark 9:47 (NAB).

[7] *Fatima in Lucia's Own Words: Sister Lucia's Memoirs*, ed. Louis Kondor, trans. Dominican Nuns of Perpetual Rosary (Cambridge, MA: Ravengate Press, 1976), 104-105.

we do not. This is how we choose to be united with Christ. This is how our actions speak louder than words. This is how we accept Christ and His promise of eternal life. We cannot accept the invitation to follow Christ into heaven, and then not follow Christ here on earth. We must put into action what we claim to be our greatest desire.

A few years ago, I was teaching a classroom of third graders about salvation. It was a heavy topic for their age, but they were very concerned about heaven and hell, even before I arrived. The teacher felt uncomfortable with Church teaching since most of us avoid even thinking about this topic, so I stepped in to help. I explained to the kids that death and being away from God is the price for sin. Jesus died to pay the price for our sins and the sins of the world. The gates of heaven are now open. All we have to do is accept the invitation. Then I asked for a show of hands to see who wanted to go to heaven. They all raised their hands, of course. I then explained that heaven is about being with Jesus and the saints forever. "Do we really want to be with Jesus? After all, Jesus is the best! Though we can have lots of fun and laughter, remember that we will have to be on our best behavior. We would never want to sin in front of Jesus. That would be disrespectful. We want to act like saints. Even if we do not do a perfect job at this, Jesus knows that we are sincerely trying. So, do you still want to go to heaven?" Of course, they did, so I followed up with, "Prove it. Prove you want to be with Jesus. What will you do, even now, that would totally convince anyone that you want to go to heaven?" The children gave all the right answers to my question, but they were not quite done with their own questions.

They asked, "Then who would go to Hell?" I explained, "Believe it or not, there are some people who do not want to be with Jesus. He will never force you to stay with Him and would be very sad if you did not accept His invitation. But, he will respect your decision. So, where do they go? If there is only heaven, there would be no place where we could go to avoid being with Jesus. So God made a place where people can be separated from Him. It is a sad, lonely, dark place with no joy. I would not recommend going there. Though some people claim they don't want to go there, their actions continue to say that they don't want to be with Jesus. So, tragically, some people choose to go to hell. I can't imagine choosing Hell, could you? Once again, a show of hands of who wants to be with Jesus in the happiness of heaven forever and ever? Then prove it by the way you live your lives."

SUICIDE

Many people have questions about **Suicide** and salvation. On the one hand, suicide is murder and a grave sin. On the other hand, family and friends of a person who had committed suicide are looking for the Church to offer hope in the midst of what may be the worst of tragedies. The first answer to the survivors is academic but comforting. As discussed in chapter six, mortal sin requires three parts: 1) gravity of the sin, 2) full awareness that it is a grave sin, and 3) freedom in choosing to sin gravely. It is clear that suicide is a grave matter, and we all recognize it as such, so the first two requirements point to suicide being a mortal sin. The third point is where there is doubt. Mentally healthy people do not contemplate, let alone commit, suicide. It is safe to assume that the person was mentally unhealthy at the time of his decision to end his own life. Mental illness reduces a person's **culpability** because he may not have been completely free in his choice. This means that there is a possibility that it was not a mortal sin, only a grave venial sin. Unlike mortal sin, venial sin does not put our salvation in jeopardy. Since we do not know the level of culpability of each person suffering from mental illness, we assume God's mercy. Therefore, we hope in forgiveness and salvation.

On the other hand, though the above academic response is comforting, it may not be the best approach for the general public. The fear of condemnation has saved many lives in the moment of suicidal temptation. Since we do not know who may eventually struggle with suicidal thoughts, the best practice is to teach people that suicide is a grave sin and puts the soul in danger of condemnation. Since only God can judge how culpable a person is in making the decision to commit suicide, the answer is unclear if this situation constitutes a "mortal sin." The circumstances are known only to God, not even the individual who contemplates suicide knows. Suicide is always sinful and always grave; circumstances known only by God determines whether it is a mortal sin.

We often overlook one important aspect of the reality of **Final Judgment:** our lives really matter. What we do in life matters to God. How we treat each other and grow in holiness matters to God. How we imitate Christ matters to God. This is very good news. Otherwise, we might think life is just a distraction before death. We might look at the pains and struggles of life as a cruel joke. Why did

God not just create us already forgiven and in heaven? Why do we have to plow our way through the daily grind if we are all just going to end up in the same place anyway? This, of course, is the main concern of the book of Ecclesiastes.[8] The promise of heaven had not yet been revealed to the author of the book of Ecclesiastes, Qoheleth. He thought that, whether we are good or bad, wise or foolish, we all end up in the grave. It was a depressing thought. But now, with the revelation of the final judgment, we can rejoice in the fact that these days are not meaningless. The way we live is the way we choose to be united with Christ or not. Choose wisely. Your immortal life depends on the decisions of your mortal life.

We do want to avoid the **Pelagian Heresy** that claims that we have to earn heaven.[9] No matter how good we are or how much sin we avoid, we still need a Savior. Going to heaven depends completely on Jesus and not on our good works, but we do have to choose Christ daily in order to receive this gift. Since we are dependent on Christ to go to Heaven, we can only go to Hell if we intentionally choose not to accept God's gift of salvation. We cannot make a mistake and end up in Hell. If we sincerely seek to be united with Christ, even if we do not know His name, Christ will do the rest.

Choosing Christ is not as easy as saying a simple sentence or doing the occasional nice deed. It requires a total commitment to the conversion process. The **Old Self** is the way we lived and thought before we committed to Christ. It is a mindset of selfishness and

---

[8] Ecclesiastes 1:2 (NAB).

[9] *The Catholic Encyclopedia*, s.v. "Pelagius and Pelagianism."

short term, worldly goals. As we begin to take seriously our commitment to the conversion process, we soon recognize that it will take time and energy to fully change. The **New Self** is a work in progress. We will often be tempted to slide back to our old, sinful habits. "Your enemy, the devil, is prowling, like a roaring lion, looking for someone to devour. Resist him, steadfast in your faith!"[10] The goal is perfection, though we know we will probably fall short. However, taking one step toward Christ is enough to accept what He is offering. He will do the rest.

Though we continue to strive for perfection, we will never be perfect in this life. We will always need Jesus. At the same time, the standard is set very high. If we are to walk with saints, we must go beyond the common kindness and politeness of the culture. Everyone knows that we are to love our families. Christ calls us to love our enemies. Everyone knows we should do favors for those who can pay us back. We are to help those who can never repay us. When we are pressed into service for one mile, we are to give two miles.[11] Think about what Jesus is saying. We are called to stand out in the world as being especially holy. It is not enough to simply blend in with everyone else. We cannot become complacent with being as good as others. We must push ourselves every day to grow, stretch, and reach for heaven. St. Paul explains that **Competing Athletes** give up all kinds of things and work tirelessly toward their goals.[12] In the end, they receive only a little symbol of their achievement. But we are working for the greatest reward: Paradise. Thus, we should work

---

[10] 1 Peter 5:8b-9 (NAB).

[11] Matthew 5:41 (NAB).

[12] 1 Corinthians 9:25 (NAB).

just as hard as athletes do to reach our goals. Run, and run so as to win the prize!

EMOTIONAL UPS AND DOWNS

After an event like a retreat, it is normal to be on a spiritual high as we set our goals for holiness. That high is often followed by a low when we realize how much work we have to do. We become aware of vices, addictions, spiritual pitfalls, traps of the Tempter, and all kinds of sins that we were not able to see before beginning the conversion process. The reason we see these sins is because we are no longer comparing ourselves to the **Lowest Common Denominator**, the most outrageous of sinners. After a retreat, we are standing in the light of Christ, the Holy One, Who deserves a better disciple. We no longer find solace in the idea that "At least I'm not a murderer." Now we find ourselves burdened with the idea that "I am no Mother Teresa."

It can be overwhelming and frustrating to realize how much we must change in order to be holy. So as not to get overwhelmed, just take "**Bite-sized pieces.**" Set small, achievable goals. One by one, renounce the vices, develop the virtues, and become the disciple God knows you can be. There have been occasions when I do not merely wait for a person to ask to go to Confession. Instead, I invite them to go to Confession. Even though people like to joke that their "Confession would take too long," it never takes as long as they think. It may seem like we have committed a lot of sins, but most of them fall under just a few categories: Lust, lies, anger, etc. The more we confess, the better we get at naming our deeper sins. Start with a few basic vices and get them out of the way.

Stick to the plan, despite the feelings of despair. Trust the Lord. You are only experiencing the fear of the Tempter who senses he is losing the battle for your soul. He will throw all kinds of obstacles in your way, reminding you of how unworthy you are and how impossible the task is. On your part, do not listen to the Tempter. He is perishing, and he knows it. Jesus said, "I have observed Satan fall like lighting from the sky!"[13] For your part, keep your eyes on Christ. Every time you are hit with the idea that you are unworthy, reply in your heart with, "That is how awesome my God is. Lord, Your love is more powerful than my worst sins. Your salvation is the light in the darkness." When you are confronted by the thought that the road to holiness seems endlessly long, remember Jesus saying, "For human beings this is impossible, but for God all things are possible."[14] When you feel weak and want to hide back in your younger days of ignorance when you could not see these sins, remember Jesus saying, "Father, they are your gift to me. I wish that where I am they also may be with me."[15] "No one takes them from my hand."[16] "I pray not only for them, but for those who will believe in me through their word."[17] Jesus is praying for you! Can you have any fear?! You are in a battle for more than your life; it is your soul that

---

[13] Luke 10:18 (NAB).

[14] Matthew 19:26 (NAB).

[15] John 17:24 (NAB).

[16] John 10:28b (NAB).

[17] John 17:20 (NAB).

is in the balance! In the words of Churchill, "We will fight on the beaches, we shall fight on the landing grounds, we shall fight in the fields and in the streets, we shall fight in the hills; we shall never surrender!"[18]

Sometimes we like to let ourselves off the hook too easily. We say things like, "I'm only human," or, "I'm no saint." Yes, we are all sinners, but the whole point of God becoming human was to raise the dignity of humanity. Christ is fully human, and thus He redefines what it means to be "only human." We are capable of much more than we think. The witness of the saints shows us that it is possible to imitate Christ, despite our human weakness. If they can do it, so can we. The saints were not superhuman. They were just regular people who took seriously the call to holiness. They worked and struggled and fought through their limitations to learn how to live as the disciples Christ deserves.

In the end, I have to admit that the saints all cheated! That's right, they cheated. Finding themselves unable to grow beyond small increments, the saints gave up on trying to become holy by their own willpower. Instead, they regularly called upon God to give them the Divine blessings that helped them become more than they could be otherwise. They asked God to do for them what they could not do for themselves. Not only is this the key to spiritual success, but it may also be the whole point of being "just human." We must rely on the grace of God to make us holy saints.

---

[18] Winston Churchill, *Winston S. Churchill: His Complete Speeches 1897-1963,* ed. Robert Rhodes James (New York, NY: Chelsea House Publishers, 1974), 6231.

Ask yourself, "Is it so bad to desire to become a saint?" Perhaps it would be pride or selfishness to desire to become famous or have the power to perform miracles for your own benefit. Yet, simply desiring to be a regular, everyday, humble saint is the **Universal Call to Holiness**. Holiness is not meant for a few special people. We are all called to become imitators of Christ, inspirations for others, and prayerful practitioners of virtue, avoiding sin at all times. Aim high and even if you fall short, you will not have long to go.

PURGATORY

What about **Purgatory**? It is true that purgatory is not directly found in the Bible. It is a logical construct theologians describe as a process of becoming worthy of the presence of God.[19] It makes a lot of sense if you think about it. Heaven is a perfect place, but how can it be so great if it has people like me in it? Like the old line goes, "I would never join a club that accepts people like me."[20]

Imagine your first day in heaven. All the angels and the saints are around you. They are beautiful. Their hair, clothing, skin, teeth, weight, everything is absolutely perfect. The ceiling, walls, floor, and windows are elegant and breathtaking. The Virgin Mary is here! She is even more radiant than you had imagined. Rose petals pale in comparison. Then there is Christ, the Face of God! If your heart were not resurrected, it would have stopped from the shock of His glory. How do you feel in the midst of all of this beauty? If you are

---

[19] *Catechism of the Catholic Church*, paragraph 1030-1032.

[20] Groucho Marx, *Groucho and Me* (New York: Bernard Geis Associates, 1959), 321.

like me, you probably feel… ugly. It is like spending an evening with supermodels. We cannot help but be so concerned with our split ends, our calloused feet, our extra pounds, our blotchy skin, our dirty fingernails. Do you know what you need? **A Heavenly Makeover.**

So often we think of purgatory as a place, like a waiting room. Worse yet, we think of it as being a punishment for not being worthy of heaven. Therefore, we assume it involves suffering as if it were some type of "hell-light." But this is not an accurate picture of what Purgatory is. It is more like a process of making your soul beautiful and ready for heaven.

Throughout our lives, we try to correct our Old Selves to become the New Creation. Some people are more successful than others in shedding their sinful habits and ways of thinking. So long as we are sincere in our efforts, we believe that Christ will provide the rest. Yet, we do not want to go to the Divine Wedding Feast underdressed.[21] The Heavenly Makeover is the process through which God re-creates us into the essence of our goodness. God re-forms His holy Image in us. I suppose it may include some discomfort, just like physical procedures to improve our beauty. It may be hard to let go of some of those old sins. Many of those sins have been life-long "friends." If we were to die still not fully converted, we pray that God would not abandon us. Just as the saints have taught us, no matter how hard we try and how much time we have on Earth, we still need Jesus in the end.

---

[21] Matthew 22:12 (NAB).

Now imagine that first day in Heaven again, but this time it is after you go through purgatory. Entering heaven will be a completely different experience after our Heavenly Makeover. We will feel like we belong. We will be as beautiful as everyone else. We will stop worrying about ourselves and start focusing on the Paradise that surrounds us. Now we recognize that purgatory is not to be feared. In fact, I am depending on it. Besides, no one goes to purgatory who is not heading toward heaven. I often pray, "Lord, whatever it takes to be with you, I am willing to do. Give me the strength to endure hardship, temptations, and suffering. If it be necessary, I embrace even going to purgatory for as long as you see fit. So long as I have the promise that it will lead to you, I gratefully accept it all."

We should not wait until death to begin the Heavenly Makeover. Right now, we can begin to change. It is our duty to do all we can to get ready to be in the presence of the Lord. He deserves a better disciple than me. I intend to become a better disciple for Him.

In heaven, there are no resentments, bitterness, or shame. Yet, it is not uncommon for us to carry around these things while here on Earth. In preparation for heaven, I have to be healed of these things. I aim to do my best while in this world, but whatever I fail to accomplish before death will have to be purified in purgatory. The problem is that these flaws involve real people, with real issues, and they are people who are really hard to love. These people are all part of a spiritual concept I call the "**Purgatory Pool.**"

The Purgatory Pool is a hypothetical construct that reminds me that I still have to progress in my spiritual life in preparation for heaven. In my Purgatory Pool are the people to whom I have been unfair or who have been unfair to me. For whatever reason, we clash.

I have a hard time forgiving them or seeking forgiveness from them. Jesus told us that we are supposed to love our enemies. While most of us think we have no enemies, we might be exaggerating the term "enemy" so as to exclude ourselves from the need to change. While we might not have an "archenemy," we all have people we find difficult to love. I am a very patient, understanding, and forgiving man. Even I have people in my Purgatory Pool. The goal is to find ways to make peace with these people and/or make amends for how we treated them.

Imagine being on a long bus trip while sitting next to *that person.* You know who *that person* is. You are sitting together, and he is being his typical annoying self. The trip seems to be taking longer than you expected. There are no open seats to switch to and you want nothing better than to get off this bus. Here is the catch: the bus arrives at the destination when you have made your peace with this person. Not a minute sooner.

Ask the Holy Spirit to show you who is in your Purgatory Pool. With whom do you need to make peace? Make a list. Now, ask the Holy Spirit to heal you of the resentments, jealousies, hurt, anger, bitterness, or shame that you experience because of this person. Next, ask the Holy Spirit to help you discover how to make your peace and, if necessary, your amends.

For the record, it is not very kind to reveal who is in your Purgatory Pool. Do not spread your discontent. Sometimes we call it "venting," it is really just an attempt to justify our negative feelings and rationalize not fixing the relationship. Under the guise of "venting," we try to rally as many people to our side of the issue as possible, isolating the other person. You know that you are merely sinning when you become defensive to anyone who does not agree with you. A spiritual director may be a safe outlet for expressing negative feelings and receiving constructive criticism.

PEOPLE ARE PATIENT WITH YOU, TOO.

The odds are that you are in someone else's Purgatory Pool. Perhaps you feel perfectly fine and have moved on from some difficult situation with a person. Perhaps you are unaware that someone finds you annoying and difficult to love. If someone comes to you asking forgiveness for a past offense, take that moment seriously. Just as we must become very humble to make peace with others, recognize the humility of anyone who wants to make peace with you. Be gentle. Say the words, "I forgive you," even if the past offense did not bother you. They need to hear your words of forgiveness so that they can forgive themselves.

When I was in my second year at the seminary, I commented to the rector that I thought the faculty should serve the food in the cafeteria instead of waiting to be served by the seminary staff. The rector told me that my comment was sinful because I was speaking judgmentally about things I did not know. I was unaware of all the charitable work the faculty was doing. He was absolutely right, but, at the time, I felt justified in my comment. Years later, I saw the rector serving the food in the cafeteria. I felt embarrassed and ashamed I had judged him. Still more years went by before I finally went to him and told him I had been unjustly judged by someone else. It reminded me that I never asked him to forgive me for my grievance against him all those years ago. He had completely forgotten about the incident but was gracious enough to forgive me. Not only did that bring healing to me as I forgave myself, but it also softened my heart toward the person who misjudged me. I made the same mistake that person did, and probably more than once.

INTERCESSORY PRAYER

Before I write about praying for the souls in Purgatory, a note about **Intercessory Prayer**. Sometimes non-believers criticize the act of praying for other people. For those who do not believe in a spiritual reality, prayer is merely a mental exercise with no benefit. At best, it appeases the worries of the mind. At worst, it prevents real action toward practical solutions to the world's problems. As believers, we know that there is power in praying for each other. In ways that we do not pretend to fully understand, the act of praying with and for each other makes a difference in the here-and-now. This has been a long-standing part of our Tradition, stretching back to before Abraham. Christ Himself prayed to the Father for our benefit,[22] giving us the supreme example of what we are expected to do. If you accept Jesus as the Messiah, then you must obey His commands and imitate His life.

There have been innumerable accounts of prayers being answered. A critic might say that the result was bound to happen whether you prayed or not. That is possible, but it is not our belief. We believe that God answers prayers, even if it is in ways we were

[22] John 17:9 (NAB).

not expecting. When a prayer is answered, it causes us to be grateful, to be reminded of God's love and compassion, and to be more dedicated to prayer. When the critic says, "Who's to say it was your prayer that made the difference?" we might respond, "Who's to say it wasn't?"

I think there is some validity in the criticism that praying for someone is not a substitute for actively doing something to help them. St. James gave the teaching that it is not helpful to merely tell someone to go on their way with a prayer that they will find the support they need somewhere else.[23] Instead, we should help them ourselves. Prayer should evoke in us a desire to serve. It should stir our creativity to find solutions and understand our role in other people's lives. At the same time, we cannot do everything. In some circumstances, we pray for someone to receive help from the right person at the right time, even if it is not us. A teenage daughter may require good counsel about her boyfriend. Though her mother has told her a million times not to allow her boyfriend to treat her so poorly, the advice falls on deaf ears. If the daughter will not listen to her mother, it is time to pray that God places in the girl's life the right person from whom she will accept good counsel. If we can help, we should. If we cannot, we pray that God sends the right person for the job. And if God sends us, we may be the answer to someone else's prayers.

Another criticism of Intercessory Prayer is, "God will do whatever He desires to do. What makes you think that you can change God's plans by begging Him? If it is good, wouldn't God want to do

[23] James 2:14-17 (NAB).

it anyway, even without your prayers?" The answer may seem simplistic to a non-believer, but it all comes down to Revelation. First, Jesus told us to knock, and said that, if we did, He would answer.[24] He wants us to pray. Secondly, the teachings of theologians, like St. Thomas Aquianas, claim that God never "changes His mind," since God would have already thought of the perfect response and, therefore, there is no need for improvement with a different plan. However, God is inviting us to participate in the planning. In the inspired Word of God in the Sacred Scriptures gives many examples where the Divine Plan seems to have taken into account the good that happens through intercessory prayer. My favorite example is the story of Moses and the **Second Copy of the Ten Commandments.**[25] Please excuse my version of the story:

Moses went up Mount Sinai a second time. God said, "Moses? I wasn't expecting you back so soon. What news do you bring me about my people? Did they like the Commandments I gave you?"

Moses responded rather sheepishly, "Yeah, about that. You wouldn't happen to have another copy of those laying around anywhere, would You?"

God's Voice became indignant, "Now, don't tell me you lost them! Those are a great gift for the people. I have spelled out for them what pleases me and what does not please me. It is a road map to blessings!"

Moses interrupted, "No, that's not it. They're great. Really. I didn't lose them. I kind of... broke them."

---

[24] Matthew 7:7 (NAB).

[25] Exodus 32:31-34:9 (NAB).

God was confused, "Did you drop them? You always were a klutz!"

With much fear, Moses explained, "No, I threw them… at an idol… that the people made when I was delayed in returning to them."

God said, "That's it! I've had it with these stiff-necked people. You know what? I'm going to call down fire from heaven and start over. I'll just wipe them out, and you and I, Moses, will go off and form a new people worthy of the title, 'My Chosen Ones.'"

Moses seemed underwhelmed with the plan as he said, "That's fine, Lord. You can do what You want. You're God, after all. I'm just saying…"

God grew impatient, "What are you saying? Spit it out already!"

Moses finally said, "Well, what would the Pharaoh think?"

God was again confused. "What does the Pharaoh have to do with this?"

Moses explained, "Well, You did go through all the trouble of the Plagues of Egypt and splitting the Red Sea. The Pharaoh will now think You did all that for nothing. He'll think You dragged the Israelites out here just to kill them. I'm just saying, it doesn't go well for Your reputation."

God considered Moses' argument for what seemed like a long time. Moses thought he might have said too much. Then, God broke the silence by saying, "I like the way you think, Moses. So be it. The people can live. But let it be known that it was because you interceded on their behalf that I held back my wrath. Now, let me get you a fresh copy of My Law, with some extra emphasis on the First Commandment."

Although my rendition is intentionally comical, it is, more or less, what is described in Exodus. Moses interceded, and God changed His plan. This and other examples in the Bible teach us that our Intercessory Prayers do make a difference. I do admit that it is still quite mysterious. Nonetheless, my trust in the Tradition of the Church handed on to us from generations before us, the accumulation of the wisdom of our people, tells me to pray for others. So I pray for everyone who asks for prayers. I name them and their causes. I am specific about my hopes. I often pray with people at the moment they ask for prayers. And I ask other people to pray for me.

As far as praying for the souls in purgatory, it has been argued that the dead are now in the hands of God and are no longer in need of prayer. After all, prayer cannot change these people or their predicament. While all of this seems logical, I still refer to the Bible. In the Second Book of Maccabees,[26] we find a military general sending a donation to the Temple to pray for the forgiveness of the souls of those who had died in sin. This passage gives me a reason to believe in **Prayer for the Dead**.

My thought is this: If my prayers have a mysterious spiritual power in this world, perhaps they do in purgatory too. I know that God's mercy does not require help from my Intercessory Prayer. If God has placed people in heaven, they are no longer in need of help from me. If they are in hell, all the prayers in the world will not save them. But, if they are in purgatory, there is a chance that I can help them in some way, though I do not know how it will help. Again,

[26] 2 Maccabees 12:43 (NAB).

God does not need my prayer to save the person. If God has determined that a soul needs time in the process of the Heavenly Makeover of purgatory, so be it. At the same time, it would be quite an honor, a truly wonderful opportunity, to be able to help someone pass through the gates of heaven. Perhaps it would be no greater than holding the door for someone already capable of opening the door himself. Yet, if I could do that for a loved one, that would be a wonderful honor that pleases me to no end.

Since heaven and purgatory are outside of time and space, perhaps my prayers can even affect souls who have already passed into heaven. Retroactively, I might be of assistance for when they were in purgatory. Imagine that I offer a prayer for the soul of my grandfather. He died sixteen years before I was born. Maybe for grandpa, it feels like the last day of purgatory and the first day of heaven. Maybe on that day, a message comes through, "Your grandson has offered a prayer for your soul." How surprised would my grandfather be? A grandson, who he never knew, helped him. He would learn that I am a priest, that his daughter raised me well, that the Faith continues in his family, and that he is remembered with love and devotion. What a great gift that would be! Maybe praying for the souls in purgatory is just a gift from God. God permits us to participate, as insignificantly as it may be, in the salvation of the souls of our loved ones. God is good!

Sometimes we think it is somehow rude or judgmental to pray for a person who has died. We feel that we are claiming they were not good enough for heaven and have not arrived yet. I have news for you all: No one is good enough for heaven! That is the whole reason Christ came! Since we do not know who is in heaven or how long it takes, it is best to assume that everyone could use some prayers. When my grandmother was dying, she asked me to pray for her after she passed. She was very devout and holy. Trying to be pious, loving, and comforting, I told her, "Oh grandma. You won't need my prayers. You're going straight to heaven."

She grabbed my arm and sternly said to me, "You pray for me!" I apologetically agreed. I do not think that she was a great sinner. I think it was just a comfort to know that she had available to her all of the support of the Holy Church and its members. When it is my time to go, please do not forget to pray for me as well.

What is interesting is that our beloved dead are still capable of praying for us, regardless of if they are in heaven or purgatory. As a child, I remember my grandmother often praying her rosary in the rocking chair. One day, I asked her what she was doing. She told me she was praying for me. I asked her if she would pray for me the next day too. She promised to pray for me every day. I said, "No offense, Grandma, but you are old. What happens after you die? Will you still pray for me?"

With a chuckle and a look of compassion in her eyes, Grandma said, "When I die, I hope to be ever so close to the Sacred Heart of Jesus. From there, Jesus can hear me even more clearly as I pray for Michael." That gave me a lot of comfort. I still rely on those prayers. Thanks, Grandma.

FAITH WHILE GRIEVING

Is it appropriate to **Grieve the Dead**? Does our sadness indicate that we doubt God's mercy or the existence of life after this? Even

Jesus cried at the death of His friend, Lazarus. Though Jesus was fully aware of life eternal, and even aware that He was going to perform a miracle to bring Lazarus out of the tomb, the Bible tells us that "…Jesus wept."[27] In so doing, He gave us permission to grieve the dead. Perhaps grieving is part of being human. We grieve that fact that we will miss our loved ones until we see them again. We grieve that we and others will have to carry on with our lives without the help or joy of having the deceased with us. We grieve all that the dead will not be able to experience here on Earth. We grieve that they are no longer able to tie up any relationships they did not have a chance to reconcile. We grieve the human reality that we are temporary, fragile creatures in this world. We grieve our mortality and the finality of our work. We are faced with the realization that we do not have a limitless amount of time to do what we are called to accomplish. We must realign our priorities to better match the reality that, one day, we will be the one whom others will grieve. Yes, it is perfectly appropriate to grieve the dead, even for those who have faith.

SANCTIFICATION

When people are officially declared to be in heaven by the Holy Church, our relationship with them changes. We call them "**Blessed**," or, after the canonization, "**Saints**." We no longer pray for the Blessed or the Saints because they no longer need our prayers. We still ask them to pray for us.

---

[27] John 11:35 (NAB).

How does the Church determine if we are in hell, purgatory, or if we made it to heaven? We have no way of knowing if someone is in hell. Even the most wicked people might convert at the last minute without our knowledge. It is not revealed to us. We do not know where the vast majority of people are. Only God can judge them. To be officially declared Blessed or saints of the Church, there is a requirement that there be some evidence that they are in heaven. Except for a few cases, it is usually a three-part investigation. First, there is a study of the life and writings of the person to see if he is worthy of imitation. Second, there are interviews with witnesses of the person's life to see if he inspired people toward holiness. Finally, there has to be a miracle attributed to the intercession of that person. The miracle is like God giving His seal of approval. It must be well documented. In modern times, this usually involves medical records. There has to be some indication that the miracle was not a natural phenomenon, but an actual communication from heaven verifying a person's sanctity. It is like having God on the witness stand giving His professional opinion on the matter.

Today, Intercessory Prayer, especially when invoking the prayers of the saints, is highly underappreciated. We tend to think we have to handle all our problems on our own. At best, we lean on our friends, counselors, doctors, and social network. For Catholics, there is a huge deposit of grace waiting for us to use. As Christopher West described, "There is a bank account filled with a million dollars' worth of grace. And we tend to take out about fifteen cents. Use it! That is why it is there."[28] I highly recommend to those to whom I offer spiritual direction to offer Intercessory Prayer for others, ask others to pray for them, and call upon the Army of Saints.

I once had a prompting of the Holy Spirit that revealed to me, "I have never prayed alone." It seemed counterintuitive at first since I have certainly prayed by myself. On further reflection, I realized that, whenever we enter into prayer, we pray with Jesus, with the Saints, and with the whole Church. It is true: I have never prayed alone!

Sometimes when I am not feeling motivated to do my daily prayers, I imagine that there is a **Priest From India** struggling to do his prayers on the other side of the world. In my mind, I sit with him and try to motivate him to stay faithful to his prayers. In return, the exercise motivates me to complete my duty, if not for my sake, at least for the sake of encouraging my brother Priest From India.

---

[28] Christopher West, *Theology of the Body for Beginners* (West Chester, PA: Ascension Press, 2004), Cf. 44.

Chapter 8

God Stacks the Deck: Gifts to Ensure Success

How can we be successful if we do not have the tools to succeed? God provides us with all we need to live, to be holy, and to succeed. Therefore, all of our successes must be credited to our participation with God's activity, generosity, love, and mercy.

On many occasions, I have been asked if I consider myself to be a Charismatic. The term, "charismatic" is understood by many Catholics as being a spirituality focused on the acts of the Holy Spirit, the Gifts of the Holy Spirit, and the style of praise that is upbeat and emotional. I do consider myself a Charismatic. I believe that the Holy Spirit is very active in my life. I desire the Holy Spirit to guide my life even more. I desire to use God's grace and spiritual gifts in the work I do to bring about the Kingdom of God.

In our Baptism and Confirmation, we have received the Gift of the Holy Spirit. In the Sacred Scriptures, there are listings of ways the early Church recognized the activity of the Holy Spirit in their lives, both through natural and supernatural gifts. St. Paul explained that the gifts were meant to be generously offered for the mission of the Church, in praise of God and in the spreading of the Gospel. When Charismatics refer to "receiving the gifts of the Holy Spirit," the expression has three different meanings: 1) The Holy Spirit gifted through the Sacraments, 2) The awareness and consciousness of the Catholic of the promptings and activity of the Holy Spirit in their own lives, or 3) An event when a supernatural gift was manifested or first manifested, such as speaking in tongues, prophesy, or healing.

I believe I have received the gift of the Holy Spirit. I have been given the occasional spiritual gifts of Interpreting Tongues and Words of Knowledge. I want the gifts of the Holy Spirit to empower me to praise God in ways I would otherwise not be able to do. I believe that the Holy Spirit desires that I work in collaboration with others whom He has gifted. I believe that the Holy Spirit wants His Church back in His hands, and I intend to give it to Him.

That being said, I may not be the typical Charismatic. I have not been given the gift of Praying in Tongues. I am not prone to be being "Slain in the Spirit," which is when a person seems to lose control of their body and fall, limp with docility and not very conscience of the activity around them. Though I enjoy the music and style of Charismatic prayer, I do not exclusively, or even mostly, pray in this form.

Sometimes Charismatics speak of the day they became aware of the Holy Spirit in their lives or the day they first experienced one of the supernatural gifts of the Holy Spirit. They call this even "baptism in the Holy Spirit." I cannot recall the day when I was "baptized in the Spirit," though I can recall many times the Holy Spirit powerfully grabbed ahold of me, granting me insights, energy, enthusiasm, and direction. I pray over people and have often witnessed the power of the Holy Spirit, though I am not sure I do this in any way different than any other priest who blesses, anoints, or forgives people. My spiritual life has been greatly influenced by the Charismatic Renewal, though I have never been a participant in a Spirit Seminar, Crucio Retreat, or a Juan XXIII Retreat. I have been a speaker or team member of many Charismatic Retreats.

I am not a leading authority on the Charismatic Movement. I admit that my reflections on the gifts of the Spirit may be relatively unrefined. Perhaps others will be able to add to this section of my writing to help mature these insights. Despite all the ink that has been poured out to explain the Charismatic Gifts and recent activity of the Holy Spirit, I think it is more accurate to say, "We are all in deep waters now." There is a great mystery happening that we do not fully understand. I offer these reflections as a means of considering more deeply the marvels of the unfolding of Pentecost and the promise that Christ will be with us to the end of time.

CHARISMATIC GIFTS OF THE SPIRIT

The Gifts of the Spirit are given to the Church and its members as a grace to help them accomplish God's Holy Mission. Without

God's grace, it would not be possible to participate in God's Plan of Salvation. Therefore, the Charisms, or special natural or supernatural gifts that God has given to individual people, are an essential tool for the Church.

Typically, the Church lists the seven Gifts of the Spirit from Isaiah 11:2-3, which are wisdom, understanding, good counsel, piety, fortitude, knowledge, and fear of the Lord. These gifts are offered in Baptism and in "fullness" through the Sacrament of Confirmation. They are permanent and offered to all the baptized. They are meant to help every Catholic live out their vocational calling to holiness.[1]

The Charismatic Gifts, or spiritual gifts, are found on two different lists: 1 Corinthians 12:1-11 and 1 Corinthians 12:28. All of these gifts are meant to be used for the benefit of others, not merely one's own sanctification. The first list seems to be supernatural, including speaking in tongues, interpretation of tongues, words of wisdom, words of understanding, healing, works of miracles, discernment of spirits, and supernatural faith. The second list seems to include natural gifts given in greater concentration, such as teaching, administration, speaking different languages, helpers, and pastoral (apostolic). Everyone is not granted these gifts at all times, nor are they necessary for personal sanctification. However, if the gifts are offered, they are to be used at the service of the Church.[2]

We should not judge a person's holiness based on whether or not they have any of the Gifts of the Spirit. These gifts are freely and

---

[1] *Catechism of the Catholic Church*, glossary, "Gifts of the Holy Spirit."

[2] *Catechism of the Catholic Church*, glossary, "Charism."

undeservedly given to people according to God's Will. The Gifts of the Holy Spirit are not dependent upon the moral goodness of the recipient. The source of the power is always God, not the person wielding the gift. If a person prays over someone and he is healed of his infirmity, praise and thanks should be given to God, not to the one who prayed. If a person is unable to speak in tongues, it should not be concluded that he is lacking in faith.

Apparently, in Corinth, St. Paul's community was divided and confused about status and levels of holiness because of the variety of gifts.[3] St. Paul chastised them for trying to claim superiority over one another based on gifts they received without deserving them. He then explained that each person is given a gift for the purpose of serving the greater Church. Receiving a gift should empower service. Also, no one person has all the gifts. The variety of gifts spread among the community encourages the members to work together toward the Mission of the Church. The more harmoniously they work together, the more they represent the Church as the Mystical Body of Christ. Just as a body has many parts that function together, each member of the Church does his part for the whole community, while relying on the other members to do their part. Each part is important to the whole. "The eye cannot say to the hand, 'I do not need you,' nor again the head to the feet, 'I do not need you.'"[4]

---

[3] 1 Corinthians 12:4-5 (NAB).

[4] 1 Corinthians 12:21 (NAB).

It can be beneficial to look at the gifts listed in 1 Corinthians 12: 1-11 with more detail. Since these gifts are manifesting within charismatic groups, it is worth exploring what they mean and how they should be used.

I liken the **Gift of Tongues** to the way an infant tries to speak. It reaches down to a language before words. It is freeing for people who pray in tongues. They consciously try to think less and just respond to God's grace. They enjoy being in God's hands, allowing the Holy Spirit to do the praising. It can be liberating to allow the grace of God to move so freely, without trying to find the words or develop their rational thinking. It is just pure prayer and submission to God. Usually, those praying do not even know what is being said. They simply enjoy the moment and let God do whatever He wants to do through them.

The purpose of the Gift of Tongues seems to be to give evidence of the presence and activity of the Holy Spirit. For some people, it is very reassuring and inspiring. For others, it can be very disturbing and unsettling. For those who are not comfortable with the Gift of Tongues, I assure you that it is not insanity or hysteria. I also assure you that God will not force this gift upon you. Unless you are open to receiving the gift, you will not suddenly begin talking in gibberish.

I have been given the **Gift of Interpretation of Tongues**. When I hear people speaking in tongues, though it sounds like gibberish, sometimes I can understand the meaning of their prayer. The words pop into my mind. I discovered my gift on a few occasions when I was able to understand when people confessed their sins in languages I had never studied (though I responded in English). Most occasions involved listening to people charismatically pray in tongues.

I have found two interesting insights through the use of my gift. First, not everyone who is speaking in tongues actually has the gift of speaking in tongues. Some people are imitating what they hear other people doing or are attempting to evoke the gift to begin happening in them. I do not think there is anything wrong with imitating the Gift of Tongues, so long as it is not for attention or deception. It might be a way for someone to express that they are open to the Gifts of the Spirit. In essence, the person prays that the Holy Spirit might offer the gift of tongues at this time for the good of the gathered community and the uplifting of the heart of one experiencing the presence of the Holy Spirit. They begin to utter sounds that simulate what the charismatic person has experienced in the past, hoping that the Holy Spirit will take over from that point and begin guiding the sounds they are making. To initiate this openness, the individual is consciously making the sounds and repeating a pattern that imitates the past experience. The Holy Spirit will not force a gift on the person, so openness is necessary, which is expressed through conscious utterances. However, we cannot force the Holy Spirit to offer the gift whenever we want it. Therefore, there is a docility to allowing the Holy Spirit to take over the gift of tongues if and when it serves God's will. In other words, we begin to utter sounds hoping the Holy Spirit will take over and offer the gift of tongues.

Second, for those who authentically have the Gift of Tongues, I interpret their prayers as being either praise of God or the revelation of some the prayer someone has in the depths of their heart. If they are struggling or joyful or anxious, these sounds become a way of expressing that inner prayer are handing over to God their concerns and desires. Maybe a person does not even know what to pray for. God provides the words or, at least, assures us that He understands. St. Paul writes, "The Spirit helps us in our weakness; for we do not know how to pray as we ought, but the Spirit himself intercedes for us with sighs too deep for words."[5] I have never heard any secret knowledge. For example, I interpreted one young man speaking in tongues. He asked what he was saying, and I said, "All I keep hearing repeated is, 'I give You my all, Lord. Protect me, Lord.' Does that mean anything to you?" The young man admitted he was considering a vocation to the priesthood, and he was nervous about giving his whole life over to God. It seemed as if his soul was praying better than his mind could formulate. It reminds me of the Magnificat: "My soul proclaims the greatness of the Lord."[6]

I can see how the Gift of Interpretation of Tongues is closely related to the **Gift of Words of Knowledge.** The Gift of Words of Knowledge, which I have also experienced, is when the one praying senses a message deep within his heart. This message seems to be a truth about the one for whom he is praying or about the group with whom he is praying. He might reveal that there is someone in the group that is struggling with a serious diagnosis. If there is a huge crowd, that could be a lucky guess. In a small crowd, or even one on one, it is amazing how accurate these Words of Knowledge can be when they are truly from the Holy Spirit.

---

[5] Romans 8:26 (NAB).

[6] Luke 1:46 (NAB).

Whereas Words of Knowledge reveal what is hidden in people's hearts, **Words of Prophecy** are messages from God to a person or a group. Sometimes this gift is manifested in a vision. It is like seeing a picture that needs to be interpreted. Only the person seeing it can explain the vision since it is a type of symbolic imagery intended for the one to whom it was given. Just as Christ used parables that the common person could understand, these visions will be understandable to the recipient.

The message of Words of Prophesy is usually a call to prayer, a renewal of confidence in the Lord, or a recognition that the Lord knows what we are going through. Sometimes it is a promise of healing. Though I am certain that this gift can be authentic, I get nervous when there are too many predictions about future events or when the words give instructions about what people ought to do. It seems to me that people can, inadvertently, "put **words into God's mouth**" to match their agenda or give someone hope through wishful thinking. Nonetheless, it is not uncommon for certain predictions of health and conflict resolution to come true.

To ensure that the messages received are authentically from God and not confused with other voices within the mind of the speaker, it is important to have a charismatic group affirm the messages heard. Whether or not the revelation is authentic, the charismatic group can consider the truth of the statement. A charismatic group should not immediately give authority to messages they have received, assuming these are authentic instructions from the Divine. The message itself must be discerned with Public Revelations given to the Church. If a person shares a message, the members of the group should acknowledge that they, too, have received the same message or that the message rings true to the Christ they know and love. If there are no affirmations, it may mean that the message was off. Perhaps the person did not word it correctly. Perhaps he put words into God's mouth. Whatever the case, the charismatic group should not judge the person for what appears to have been a mistake. The prayer group should be a safe place to develop and practice the use of our spiritual gifts. Remember, we are all in deep water now. None of us fully understands this mystery of the activity of the Holy Spirit.

The **Gift of Healing** is a powerful working of the Holy Spirit that can be manifested in either physical healing or spiritual healing. It is good to ask for healing. It is loving to pray for someone who wants healing. It is proper to rejoice over one who has received healing. At the same time, physical healings are all temporary. Even the people Jesus healed eventually got sick and died. Therefore, while physical healing is great and fills people with hope and awe, a less recognizable spiritual healing is an even greater gift because it will last into eternity.

The complications with the gift of healing are many. First, it is possible to give false hope that healing is taking place when it is not. Second, a pious person may try to show their confidence in the gift of healing by ignoring medical attention. Jesus, Himself, healed with different methods. Sometimes He merely said a word.[7] On another occasion, He put clay on the eyes of the blind man.[8] Who are we to tell God that He must use miracles rather than medicine to cure us?

---

[7] Luke 18:42 (NAB).

[8] John 9:6 (NAB).

Let God do it the way He wants to do it. Go to the doctor! Third, some people misunderstand a lack of healing as being a lack of faith on the part of the sick person. This judgmental approach places even more, unnecessary stress on the sick person. Fourth, critics may claim that a person was going to be healed regardless of the prayers. In most cases, healing is an unconvincing manifestation of the Holy Spirit for those who lack faith. Finally, some people might claim to have the gift of healing in order to swindle people out of their money.

It seems to me that the Gift of Healing, like all of the Gifts of the Spirit, is meant to be used in conjunction with other gifts. While the possibility of physical healing and the shocking outward sign of witnessing a healing may grab people's attention, the results are only temporary. God's priorities are, typically, long term in nature. Though it is possible that God wanted to heal people for the sake of empowering them or reminding them of His love, those goals could have been met by healings in private prayer. Using the Gift of Healing, on the other hand, is a communal act that draws people into the charismatic experience and the work of the Church. While the miracles grab the attention of the crowd, other Gifts of the Spirit should be used to further develop and mature the faith of the people. Jesus did not merely heal the sick, though many came to Him looking for healing or curiously trying to grab a glimpse of the miracle worker. Jesus used those opportunities to then teach the crowds about the Kingdom of God and to call them to conversion.

Another Charismatic experience is being "**Slain in the Spirit**." This occurs when someone prays over a person, usually placing a hand on the person's head, and the person being prayed over then falls over, semi-conscious, "resting in the Spirit." Where "slain in the Spirit" implies that the muscles have loosened and the person finds their body going limp, "resting in the Spirit" is more when the mind is no longer distracted with stray thoughts or outside distraction. The person becomes fully focused on the interior prayer life. The understanding is that the Holy Spirit has powerfully come upon the person. In total submission to the power of God, the person abandons all resistance. This causes the body to go limp and the mind to become so docile that the thoughts go blank. After this experience, many have a great sense of release of stress, joy, a new Gift of the Spirit, a healing, or a deliverance from something that had been oppressing them. Other manifestations of the same event include a sudden rush of tears or laughter. Sometimes these manifestations seem to be occurring in a crowd or a portion of a crowd, creating waves of people overwhelmed by the power of the Holy Spirit.

Charismatic gifts are purely spiritual. Other gifts are a combination of human talents with Divine Grace. This includes the gifts of administration, teaching, discernment, helps, pastoring, and evangelization. These gifts, though originating from God, can work with the natural talents of a person and be developed to maturity. They include the gifts of teaching, administration, pastoring, and I would include medicine as a participation in natural healing. These gifts are increased in their effectiveness through study, experience, and grace. Some are gifted in these areas without having faith, relying solely on their human gifts. For Christians, we participate with the grace of God, knowing that "Grace builds on nature," or as St.

Thomas Aquinas would write, "Grace does not destroy nature, but perfects it."[9]

VOCATIONS

Some people may come to a spiritual director seeking help with discerning their **Vocation** to the single life, the married life, the religious life, or the priesthood. Many people, especially if they are called to the priesthood and religious life, give witness to receiving a divine communication that prompted them to seek a specific vocation. A vocation is always an invitation from God and not a demand. It requires the ability to be properly formed in the spirituality of the vocation and the ability to meet the demands of that vocation. Additionally, the vocation needs to be affirmed by the proper authority. In the case of religious life, that would be the superior. In the case of the priesthood, it is the bishop. In the case of marriage, it is both the official of the Church and the other person to whom one wants to be married. A vocation must be a free choice. It must be a full commitment. Finally, it must be the intention of the couple that it be a life-long commitment. You cannot validly enter into a marriage if your intention is to end it due to certain circumstances, like illness, infidelity, or better prospects.

Married couples vow fidelity (chastity and monogamy), to love and respect each other, and an openness to having children. The couple will have to work on developing a communal spirituality,

---

[9] Thomas Aquinas, *Summa Theologiae*, I, Q. 1, Art. 8.

representing each other in their actions and decisions, sharing responsibilities and the struggles of life, and sacrificing personal goals for the family goals. This will require dedication to fostering a stronger relationship using a variety of techniques. Humbly, they should seek good counsel about how to do this, even before there are stresses in the relationship. In marriage, they also accept the responsibility to encourage and promote the spiritual wellbeing of their spouse through prayer, example, encouragement, and constructive criticism. They should have the utmost concern for the salvation of their spouse.

The openness to children requires further discernment about when to have children, how many children to have, and the possibility of adoption. Finances and standard of living are not the only factors, but are the most prevalent factors. There may be considerations about genetic disorders that the parents carry. The couple may be experiencing relationship stress and desire to give more attention to each other at this time for the long-term health of their relationship. There may be a sickness or injury that one of the married people needs to give resources and energy toward. There may be a national crisis of war, feminine, economic depression, etc.

Once, I asked a couple in my parish how they decided to only have two children. They admitted that it was a number they thought of before they were even old enough to get married. I suggested they pray about the decision. After all, it is only through couples that God brings human beings into existence. Every life changes history for all future generations. Because it is such a huge decision, I admire couples who allow God to be central in that discernment. Though the couple I was visiting were uncomfortable and, frankly, annoyed with my questioning, they went on to have two more children. They cannot imagine life without their four boys, two of whom would have never existed had they not prayed about their decision.

In their wedding vows, couples also promise to raise their children as Catholics, having them baptized and properly instructing them in Church teaching. This requires further discernment on how to best accomplish this task.

It is wise for married couples to continue to develop the virtue of chastity. Though they may be very much in love and committed to each other, it would be foolish for them to assume that they are stronger than others who have fallen into sin. Honesty with a spiritual director can help to curb unchaste desires and to avoid further temptations. For example, one gentleman admitted to me in spiritual direction that it was difficult to be sexually and romantically active with his wife, and then turn off those emotions when he went to work. I am less concerned about the person who talks about his struggle with chastity than I am about the person who avoids the subject. It can be helpful to work with a spiritual director to understand those feelings and the sense of conflict in one's heart. I admire those who take seriously their desire to please the Lord, even in those difficult or embarrassing conversations.

A few general rules for chastity: Sex should never be separated from love, especially with your spouse. Every act of sex should be a renewal of the commitment to love and honor each other. There should be good communication in order to ensure the expression of sexual love is being interpreted as it is intended. It will require humility, honesty, and sacrifice in order to put the emotional and sexual needs of your spouse before your own.

While being perfectly faithful to each other, married couples are obliged to share their spirituality, wisdom, loving support, and abundance with the greater community. They should stay informed about and participate in civil matters. They should influence policies and laws according to proper discernment. They should seek noble means of providing for their family.

Priests and religious make vows to live a life of prayer, to be faithful to Church teachings, and to be obedient to their proper authority. Just like any relationship, the relationship with God in a **Life of Prayer** needs to be nurtured and given attention, or it can grow stale and die. **Fidelity to Church teaching** requires not only knowing and understanding those teachings, but also giving proper reverence to the teaching authority of the Church, especially with regard to the teachings that seem most difficult to accept. Finally, the vow of **Obedience** is realized most fully when you disagree with the authority. If the proper authority makes a decision, so long as the directive is not obviously contrary to the Gospel, obedience is required, even if it is an inferior decision to yours. That obedience must be lived out with true, loving affection for one's authority. Priests and religious should pray often to grow in love and respect for their authority. The practice of obedience is related to submitting our will to the Will of God. Just as fasting can help someone regain control over bodily passions, the practice of obedience can strengthen a person to resist rebelliousness towards God.

With proper obedience and respect, it is imperative that priests and religious work with their proper authorities to ensure that the authorities are given the best information, options, and counsel to aid their decision making. It is highly recommended to pray for and with one's authority regarding discernment of God's Will.

The Single Life is a stage before we commit to a life-long vocation. However, the Single Life, too, can be a vocation of its own. It is not merely a "consolation prize" when marriage is unattainable. The Single Life can be a way to live out one's vocation in a free, fruitful, faithful, permanent, life-long state. In my extended family, the **Single Life** is not uncommon. Some people view the calling to the single life as some sort of stigma. They feel as if others had expected them to enter into another vocation. The single life can be holy, fruitful and fulfilling. Not only is it a perfectly legitimate vocation, but it is also the vocation of Jesus Himself. Though He became the archetype of the priesthood, He did not function in the profession of a Jewish priest. He was not a member of a religious community. He did not marry. He has given the single life honor and dignity. Jesus' best friends, Mary, Martha, and Lazarus, were all single. Those who are living the vocation of the single life should take note of the spiritual dangers and necessary virtues to be developed that I have listed above concerning Parish Priests who live alone.

Celibacy is considered a discipline of the Church. A "discipline of the Church" means that it is not a requirement for holiness and can be included or excluded depending on the practical duties of the members of the Church in a specific time and setting. In the case of celibacy, there have been times in history, and even in the Eastern Catholic Church today, where some priests are married. They are valid, authentic, and recognized priests without discrimination. Many people have a sense that God calls them to marriage. Follow the plan of the Lord. At the same time, there is a certain percentage of the population that, even prior to considering being a priest or a religious sister or brother, do not feel God is calling them to marriage. St. Paul would advise those who are single not to marry but, if they later decide to marry or engage in normal sexual relations with their spouse, they do not commit a sin.[10] While it is not, strictly speaking, a requirement for priesthood, only celibate men are currently being called to the priesthood in the Roman Catholic Church. Upon ordination, priests are to remain celibate. The Holy Father has the authority to change the requirement that only celibate men can be ordained as priests if there is a practical benefit to abandoning the discipline. This would not mean that current priests could get married. They have already committed themselves to celibacy and are already in a fatherly relationship with other people. Even those married priests in the Eastern Catholic Church are not allowed to remarry if their spouse were to pass away. This would create a conflict with their proper relationship with the flock. It is inappropriate for a pastor to court a parishioner due to the inequality of roles.

When I was a seminarian, a missionary gave me the advice, "Do not pray to endure celibacy; pray to embrace it." Celibacy is a way of loving by being less focused on my wants and needs, and more focused on the needs of the greater community and on the Mission of the Church. Celibacy provides a great freedom to be fully committed to the promptings of the Holy Spirit, regardless of the sacrifices that may be required. Because of celibacy, I am free of the concerns of providing for a family, their education, their housing, and their involvement in a community. My energy, time, and resources can be

---

[10] See 1 Corinthians 7:25-28 (NAB).

directed exclusively to my ministry. This gives me the freedom to change the location of my residence or ministry with little notice, even to areas that may risk my health. I can accept professional opportunities with little consideration of being compensated. I can risk being prophetic with unpopular topics without worrying about the reputation of my family. I try to avoid thinking of it as merely dedicating more of my energy, time, and resources to my own interests. Instead, I embrace celibacy as a way of being fully dedicated to loving others.

I believe that celibacy is a very powerful witness of dedication and trust in the Mission of the Church. For most young people, the first concern raised by religious life is celibacy. They see it as a great sacrifice. To be clear, it is a great sacrifice, but not impossible or miserable. The young are amazed, and sometimes incredulous, that anyone would sacrifice something our culture considers so important. They wonder how a person can be happy or fulfilled as a celibate. Underlying this mentality is some illusion that sex equals happiness. In ministering to many married couples over the years, I have realized that sex, though good and pleasurable, is not as important as the young think it is. Nonetheless, accepting celibacy instead of seeking the natural desire for carnal pleasure is seen as a powerful witness. The culture sees a commitment to celibacy as a strong, sacrificial, even heroic sacrifice for God.

Despite what the culture tells us, no one has ever died from a lack of sex. The body has natural desires for sex, but these are only desires, not needs. In our culture, there is an overemphasis on satisfying all of our desires, oftentimes instantaneously. Part of the life of simplicity is to recognize how little we actually need. As we deny our bodily desires, we fortify our willpower. With a fortified will, we are better able to defend against temptation. In a simplified life, we come to appreciate the little things all the more. We do not move past them too quickly, seeking our own satisfaction. We savor intimate friendships, kind gestures, and beauty, even more, when we have learned not to indulge our desires too quickly. Also, sacrificing desires helps to free us from becoming attached to or dependent on worldly things. The day may come when we are faced with a choice between God's Will and our own desires. If we are not free enough from our attachments, we cannot choose to follow the Lord. Imagine a prisoner of war who is tortured for information. With sufficient practice of personal sacrifice prior to his being captured, the prisoner will be willing to endure all kinds of hardships without giving over the location of his fellow soldiers. Think of St. Maximillian Kolbe who gave his life for the sake of another prisoner.[11] Sufficiently free from the "need" of our attachments, we will be free to choose the greater spiritual good over and above the worldly goods and pleasures.

In addition to the previously mentioned promises, members of some religious communities take a **Vow of Poverty**. This has its own spirituality connected to solidarity with the poor, simplicity of life, and dependence on God. It is an excellent witness to being fully committed to sacrificing one's desires for the sake of the Divine Plan. Years ago, I visited a nursing home in Guatemala run by a religious community. The young Sisters wore no shoes. They lived an

---

[11] Sergius C. Lorit, *The Last Days of Maximilian Kolbe* (Brooklyn, NY: New City Press, 1982), 15-21.

extremely simple life as they cared for the poorest elderly patients. Many slept on mattresses on the floor. The Sisters were joyful, loving, and gentle, and they seemed very fulfilled in their lives. To this day, I am truly in awe of how little they needed to be completely happy. I pray that their joy never fades. They are a blessing to the elderly and to all those they inspire, including me.

Because of their limited access to resources, those who take a vow of poverty must defend against the temptation of greed. It has been my experience that poor people, when given a little, can become extremely greedy. They fear to lose the little they have. Religious must be careful to stay connected to the true purpose and nature of the vow of poverty.

There are other vows, such as a fourth vow of obedience to the Holy Father or a life of penance, that some religious communities take, but I have little experience of them, so I cannot comment on those other vows.

IN THE CONTEXT OF THE PARISH

Parish Priests will have to come to know the members of their congregation, discern the spiritual needs of the congregation, be creative in addressing those spiritual needs, and work in collaboration with the gifts of people both inside and outside of the parish. Parish priests must learn to sacrifice personal desires for the good of the congregation. They will need to network within the greater Church to avoid operating as a separate entity. They will have to find a balance in their ministry between doing the things that seem rewarding and energizing and performing the necessary responsibilities that can be draining.

Parish priests who live with other priests, though usually not formed in community living, will have to learn the basics of community life. This includes setting time to gather, pray, and make communal decisions, being emotionally supportive, and resolving conflicts. Parish Priests who live alone have to be careful about not living like bachelors. They must be disciplined to stay committed to their prayer life without the supervision of others. They need to develop a social network, a routine of rest and work, and a balance between being accessible and being secluded. They must be intimate, but not romantically involved, with a smaller circle of friends. They will need to be humble enough to reach out for assistance when dealing with physical, emotional, or mental health issues. They will need to continue to mature professionally by staying up with the latest studies, cultural trends, evangelization techniques, or ecclesial emphasis of the diocese or global Church. It is not acceptable to merely coast on past formation or successes. A spiritual director can be immensely helpful for a priest in staying accountable and motivated to continue developing spiritually.

DID I GET THE CALLING WRONG?

Some people have the tragic sense that their vocation was thwarted, incomplete, or unrealized. I call these **Broken Vocations**. This includes people who wanted to get married but never did, people who did not want to get divorced but did, people who were not accepted into a religious community or the priesthood, people who were prevented from doing the ministry they felt called to do, or people who made mistakes that caused them to be rejected from their vocational status. People in these categories are usually hurting and seeking spiritual healing. The wounds may cause them to feel rejected, unappreciated, worthless, lost, resentful, panicked, or a whole slew of other emotions. They may direct their pain toward God or toward whoever made the decision that changed their path of life.

As a fellow human being, a spiritual director should affirm the hurt feelings of the person. At the same time, it is important not to feed into the blame-game; that would be counterproductive. It is more helpful to set goals of recovery. Have the person begin to envision life after the Broken Vocation. Move from focusing on the past toward hopes for the future. They may not be willing to let the vocation go, quite yet. Assure them that the goal is to get healthy enough to discern God's Will properly. When they are healed, they can then make the decision to either fight to correct an injustice or to move on to another vocation.

Sometimes people may find it difficult to enter back into a trusting relationship with the Lord. They may feel that the Lord abandoned them, tricked them, or that the will of the Lord is impossible to determine. They may be afraid to risk guessing the Will of God and compounding the consequences. This is very understandable. Spiritual directors or close friends should not feel pressured in to having all the answers. Sometimes, the best we can offer is to simply accompany the person as they struggle to find healing. Pray over them often. Assure them of the good you see in them. Recognize the courage that it took for them to risk following the Lord. Feel their pain without pretending we can take it away with some secret knowledge. Sometimes, I have to admit, I do not understand why something happened. I, too, find myself wanting to blame someone. Resist this temptation. Stay with the healing.

MULTIPLE CALLINGS?

Is it possible to have two vocations? All priests, religious and married couples had originally been in the state of the single life. Much of the discernment about their worthiness to enter into the new vocation is based on an evaluation of how well they lived their first state. Deacons and some Eastern Catholic priests are married clergy, meaning they are in both the vocation of marriage and the vocation as a clergy. This can bring complications and conflicting interests and requires a special grace. St. Paul recommended that those who are single remain single, and those who are married remain married, though he expressed it was merely his opinion and not a law given to him by Christ.[12] His reasoning is based on the conflicting interests they would endure regarding family life and the work of the Church. Some people tend to manage those conflicting interests better than others. Even some Associations of the Faithful include vowed religious who are married. Therefore, it is possible to have two vocations, though it may require additional grace and effort to accomplish. For this reason, the Church has, traditionally, been very reluctant to allow married men or women to commit to a religious vocation.

---

[12] 1 Corinthians 7:25-28 (NAB).

It is beyond the scope of this book, as well as my expertise and experience, to write about the divorced and remarried, married Roman Catholic priests, or woman priests. Please forgive my reluctance to open up these cans of worms.

Chapter 9

Stay in Your Lane

This chapter is about proper training and being in a Right Relationship. We are not called to be the boss of everyone. Nor are we to accept the authority of everyone. When is appropriate to take the role of a leader, teacher, director, or guide? Who is our proper authority and why?

First of all, it is important to recognize the competency of the spiritual director. If you are not trained in psychology, medicine, counseling, or advanced spirituality, do not pretend that you are. Know when it is time to bring in someone more qualified. Recognize that people who seek good, spiritual counsel are looking for Truth (as in Jesus), not merely another opinion. We are called to pass on the Truth as it has been passed on to me from Revelation and the Tradition of the Catholic Church. There is absolutely nothing wrong with admitting that we do not have all the answers. It would be very dangerous to lead people based on our own, imagined thinking in subjects we are ill-prepared to teach.

We should avoid the tendency to treat prayer like Magic. **Magic** is the attempt to manipulate people, objects, luck, or events through spiritual practices. We must avoid the idea, no matter how pious it may seem, that a certain devotion or series of prayers is guaranteed to cause the desired result. Many traditions border on the magical. I respect them as cultural expressions from our ancestors, but I still tend to discourage practices that at least hint at magical notions. This may include burying a statue of St. Joseph in the backyard to sell a house, novenas that guarantee pregnancy, medals that protect us from worldly harm, or practices that ensure monetary prosperity. I prefer to simply pray with trust that God will provide whatever is needed for salvation. Everything else is not essential. We may express our desires, but we must always let God decide what is best for us.

This does not mean that I am opposed to religious articles, like scapulars, rings, or medals. I myself wear a ring and a medal. They are reminders, for us and for others, of our identity, which is intimately connected with the greater religious Tradition. I simply raise the caution that the objects are to help us to enter into prayer and do not have magical or salvific powers in themselves. I once met a farmer in his cornfield and invited him to Mass. He pulled out his scapular and told me, "I do not need to go to church. If I die with this on, I will go to Heaven. That is enough for me." It was a skewed version of the Tradition that concerns me greatly. There is no substitute for an authentic prayer life.

I do not know much about **Angels**. We read in the Sacred Scriptures about angelic powers, cherubim and seraphim, the Army of Angels, Ss. Raphael, Gabriel, and Michael, the Angel of Death, the angel that blocks Paradise, the angels that protect our feet from stumbling, the angel that comforted our Lord in the Garden of Gethsemane, and angels ascending and descending. There is so little revealed about their nature. There are lots of speculations about them that I do not find to be very helpful. I tend not to focus very much on that which is still unclear to Theology. One thing we do know is that angels are not other gods or demigods. They are created by the Creator and exist in a way that is mysterious to us. It suffices to think of angels as messengers of God that are signs of God's intervention in history. Beyond this, I have very little to share.

Demons are another subject that is very unclear to me. We know that Jesus helped people who were possessed.[1] We are told that demons are fallen angels. Demons manipulating us and causing suffering. It is not that divine will that we are confused and suffer. Therefore, demons are against the divine will. However, they are mere creatures. God made them. Therefore, it is the divine will that they exist, otherwise they would not. For what purpose, it is unclear, though there are speculations that they exist to test us. Did they once obey God and then misuse their free will? Even the Book of Revelation explains this relationship of demons and angels in ambiguous, symbolic, mysterious terms. One thing is clear: There is only one

---

[1] Luke 9:39 (NAB).

God. Therefore, demons are not lesser gods in a battle between good and evil. There is no comparison between mighty God and the demons. Jesus clearly had authority over the demons. We should place our trust in the one true God.

Many people suffer from demonic influences, temptations, attachments, obsessions, oppressions, and possessions. Therefore, I do not doubt that demons exist. Yet, Revelation is so vague about the nature of demons that it seems to me that most of what is written about demons is conjecture. I have little to offer on this topic except that Christ is more powerful than any demon. Our baptism protects us and gives us freedom from evil. Therefore, demons cannot influence our decisions unless we choose to let them do so. Even in temptation, we have the choice to entertain the fleeting thought, or to turn immediately back to God. Still, one glance from Christ is far more powerful than a million demons. The old say, "the devil made me do it," seems to place the blame on the devil and not accept any responsibility. Turn to the Lord. That is our duty and salvation.

Therefore, it is better to spend our energy focusing on Christ rather than on demons. However, it may benefit us to realize when we or the ones we love are afflicted by the demonic influences. This may reorient our attention to the source of our salvation and protection.

In chapter five, we have already covered attachments and obsessions. What about oppression? If a person suffers from spiritual **Oppression**, their obsessive thoughts begin to interrupt their daily lives, preventing them from seeking help. In the worst cases, there may be manifestations of seeing shadows or promptings to do evil or harmful things. For example, a person dealing with drug addiction may be suffering, not only from the physical-chemical addiction, but also a spiritual oppression. They want to be free of the addiction but are unable to escape it on their own. Their lives begin to revolve around the addiction. Spiritual oppression, much like chemical dependency, requires the work of professionals. The average spiritual director is not equipped to handle this level of spiritual slavery alone and will have to look for other support groups and experienced guides to intervene.

Spiritual **Possession** is when a person begins to lose their identity to the enslavement. They resist treatment, Truth, or prayer, despairing that they could ever be healed. They doubt the power of Christ to save or free them. Sometimes there are other manifestations that are outside of the ordinary. Individuals who are possessed may experience paranoia, hearing voices, the impulsive desire to harm themselves or others, seeing shadows in the corner of their eyes, seeing demonic figures, or objects moving on their own. The average spiritual director, including me, is unqualified to even diagnose a spiritual possession. Never accuse someone of being possessed. If a loved one is suffering from some sort of spiritual attack and your traditional prayers are not improving the situation, it is time to humbly accept that this is beyond your expertise and seek the next spiritual authority available to you. This may be your parish priest. If needed, your parish priest might need to seek an even more specialized authority. It is appropriate that the diocesan exorcist is contacted by the parish priest instead of the parishioner directly. Avoid even suggesting to the afflicted person that they need an exorcism. Let the parish priest handle it. You may make your suggestion to the priest, but we do not want the afflicted to feel ostracized or judged. I prefer the term, "Spiritual Authority delegated by the bishop." Too many movies have influenced the way people understand spiritual warfare. We do not want to add to people's fear. Try to keep the focus on Christ.

In the baptism ritual, there is the **Minor Rite of Exorcism**. While it is an optional prayer, I highly advise praying it over children and adults being baptized. It is meant to ask for God's protective hand to defend the baptized from evil influences. It is a prayer of keeping us free to love God, without fear.

I think it would be a mistake to attribute the rarity of cases of oppression, obsession, and possession simply to the advancement of psychology. I am very grateful for the advancements and proper use of psychology. For many cases, psychological and spiritual health are interwoven. Yet, I believe that the real reason for having fewer cases of spiritual enslavement is the prevalence of baptism. Most people in the United States are baptized. In 1975, 91% of Catholics were baptized. In 2022, only 64% are baptized, which is still the majority. Compare that to the fact that 68% of the world is unbaptized.[2] I find that other parts of the world where most of the population is not baptized tend to have a higher number of cases of spiritual enslavement. Exorcists in those countries are much busier than they are in the United States. Though I am sure that some cases of demonic influence were misdiagnosed psychological issues, I think that baptism

---

[2] Bruce Drake, "Number of Christians Rises, but Their Share of World Population Stays Stable," Pew Research Center, March 22, 2013, https://www.pewresearch.org/short-reads/2013/03/22/number-of-christians-rises-but-their-share-of-world-population-stays-stable/#:~:text=There%20are%202.18%20billion%20Christians,Forum%20on%20Religion%20%26%20Public%20Life.

is a major factor in the drop in cases. That being said, we should be cautious about the way we minister to the upcoming generation that has tended away from organized religion. As fewer people are baptized, more people will be susceptible to these spiritual dangers.

Ghosts are another popular topic that occasionally comes up in spiritual direction. Again, very little is revealed to us about the nature of ghosts, leading to much speculation which may or may not be true. There is little in the Bible that refer to ghosts. The Apostles thought that the Lord walking on the water was a ghost.[3] This seems to suggest that ghosts may exist, but not in the material world. Therefore, they could be purely spiritual or exist only in the mind. Some of the saints and the faithful have claimed to see people who had died. Even the Witch of Endor had a vision of the dead prophet Samuel when King Saul visited her.[4] Though it is not uncommon for someone to claim to see a ghost, it is difficult to ascertain if it was a vision in the world or in the imagination. Sight requires the refraction of light. As light bounces off physical objects, it bounces back to the eye, allowing the person to perceive shapes and colors. If a ghost has no physical body, the light will not refract. Therefore, seeing a ghost must not be an act of the eye. That being said, I do not know if ghosts exist outside of the imagination. If they do exist, I do not know why they exist. Speculations about souls trapped between realities have never been revealed in our Faith. I prefer to place my confidence in the teaching of the Church. When people tell me they

---

[3] Matthew 14:26 (NAB).

[4] 1 Samuel 28:13 (NAB).

are experiencing ghostly visions, I take them seriously, while redirecting their attention back to Christ.

There is a difference when the Tradition of the Church speaks about visions or encounters with the living, resurrected Jesus or those in the Communion of Saints. There is no sense that they are seeing ghosts, but are having a "heavenly vision," as if they were seeing beyond the physical world into a spiritual, though present, reality. The children of Medjugorje have their visions of the Virgin Mary, no one else can see what they see.[5] The Church reveres Faustina, St. Paul, and St. Anthony of Padua, and others who claim to have seen the Risen Lord, even after the Ascension. Though it may seem like the same as seeing ghosts, the Church considers these visions distinct and authentic.

I do not try **Dream Interpretation**, although this, too, is found in Sacred Scripture in the Book of Genesis,[6] the Book of Daniel,[7] and the dreams of St. Joseph.[8] Most dreams I assume are normal, subconscious processes without any further meaning. I do not worry about dreams as being premonitions or predictions of things to come. If a person is troubled or excited about a dream, I try to listen to what the dream means subjectively to the dreamer. A dream

---

[5] Svetozar Kraljevic, *The Apparitions of Our Lady at Medjugorje 1981-1983: An Historical Account with Interviews*, ed. Michael Scanlan (Chicago, IL: Franciscan Herald Press, 1984), 16.

[6] Genesis 40:8 (NAB).

[7] Daniel 4:15 (NAB).

[8] Matthew 1:20, 1:13, 1:19 (NAB).

about a bear might be scary to one person and remind another person of a teddy bear. In and of itself, the bear has no further meaning, but it may have meaning to the dreamer.

I do admit that God may speak to a person through dreams. After all, God can do anything, and He has communicated with saints through dreams. At the same time, I feel unequipped to interpret dreams. It is better for the dreamer to explain what he or she interprets as the meaning of each character and action in the dream. From there, I can pull out a new conversation about hopes and fears. If a person dreams about a car crash, I might explore how the events made the dreamer feel. Is it about being prepared for death? Or about being out of control? Or being frightened about events that seem inevitable? Then, we focus on the new topic that was drawn from the conversation about the dream. In most cases, I find the new conversation to be more fruitful than any speculations about dreams.

I strongly urge people to stay away from the **Occult**. This includes Ouija boards, fortune tellers, séances, magic spells, pagan rituals, and curses. In the Old Testament,[9] as well as in St. Paul's writings,[10] this is explicitly forbidden. Obviously, I believe in spiritual realities. By their nature, they are mysterious and outside of our full understanding. I trust in the prayers, rituals, blessings, and Revelations handed on to us through the Holy Church. It is dangerous to play with spiritual realities outside of our Tradition for two main reasons. First, we may inadvertently invite into our lives forces that

---

[9] Exodus 22:17, Leviticus 19:31, Deuteronomy 18:10-12 (NAB).

[10] Colossians 2:8 (NAB).

are not of God. Many experience obsession, or worse, after playing with such things. Second, these practices warp our way of thinking. They are often about trying to manipulate God, others, or luck. Instead of growing in our reliance on Christ and trusting in His Divine Plan, we attempt to use spiritual powers to discover hidden truths and seek our own glory. Practicing the occult is a sin that should be confessed, renounced, and not tolerated.

There are some grey areas where our culture has mixed non-Christian practices with Christian beliefs or mental health practices. These include yoga, New Age, reiki, and manipulating auras. I am uncomfortable with such practices since they deviate from Catholic Tradition. I believe they can skew our understanding of the Faith and bring confusion to the Catholic paradigm of thinking, especially with regards to anthropology. I find that these practices are pseudo-scientific, and I have no confidence in them. Though others claim that these practices are dangerous, I must humbly admit that I simply do not understand them, and I do not see how they relate to our Faith. Therefore, I discourage Catholics from practicing them.

There are some non-Christian rituals or studies that are beyond where the faithful are permitted to venture. I am not an expert in these systems of belief, and I am in no way qualified to safely navigate the interweaving of completely different belief systems. Therefore, I advise the faithful not to tinker with the practices of Hinduism, Buddhism, Native American Spirituality, Taoism, Islam, or other religions outside of the Judeo-Christian Tradition. We should also avoid religions that claim to be Christian but have very different understandings of Christ than the other Christian denominations, specifically Mormons and Jehovah's Witnesses.

I believe the study of Judaism and of other Christian denominations is acceptable so long as there is a clear dialogue with a spiritual director regarding any confusion or inconsistencies. It is insulting to the Catholic Church, as well as to the Protestant Churches, to claim that "we are all the same." It is true that we proclaim the same God. Yet, the historical and theological differences that make us distinct should be respected. For this reason, Catholics cannot substitute the attendance of a prayer service at a non-Catholic church for the Sunday Mass obligation. However, I do permit those I spiritually direct to attend the prayer services of non-Catholic churches, including weddings and funerals, so long as they do attend Catholic Mass on Sunday as well.

Catholics should not receive "communion" at non-Catholic Churches, even if they are invited to participate. The reason is partly because of our different beliefs about the Eucharist and partly because we are not in communion with the Protestant Churches. For the same reason, non-Catholics may attend Catholic Masses, but they may not receive Holy Communion. It is good that we long to be united and strongly desire to share Communion with each other. Keep praying that God may help us reconcile our differences. Until that day comes, we must hunger for healing among our brothers and sisters in Christ. We are not permitted to circumvent that healing process and take our own initiative to receive each other's Communion.

As far as participating in the Eastern Catholic Churches, I welcome and encourage those I spiritual direct to embrace the fullness that is our Universal Church. They may go to the Sacraments and pray according to the Eastern Traditions. Unfortunately, I may not be very helpful in processing their experiences since I am painfully ignorant about the Eastern Catholic Churches. Perhaps they can teach me.

The bottom line is to stay within our own competency, which is the Roman Catholic Tradition. When people are asking for spiritual advice, it is not the place for speculations and conjectures. Simply pass on the Faith as you have received it. I am reminded of the last words of St. Paul's Letter to the Galatians, "There are some who are disturbing you and wish to pervert the gospel of Christ. But even if we or an angel from heaven should preach to you a gospel other than the one that we preached to you, let that one be accursed!"[11]

---

[11] Galatians 1:6b-8 (NAB).

Appendix

Resources for Spiritual Directors

The following section includes suggested agendas for Spiritual Direction Sessions. It also includes notes the spiritual director should write following a session. These agendas are not meant to be adhered to strictly.

It is not suggested that the spiritual director share the Journey of Faith model with those they are directing, since it may give a false impression that they are being graded or judged.

This book contains many suggestions for contemplation, topics to study, discernment techniques, and penances to offer as a benefit to you and the person seeking spiritual direction. Let the Holy Spirit guide the conversation. The hope is to be able to measure progress and make meaningful steps toward established goals of spiritual maturity or healing. May we all strive to become the disciples Christ deserves.

Initial Spiritual Direction Session

1. Begin by leading an opening prayer, inviting the Holy Spirit to guide you both.
2. Tell me about yourself. Married? Children? Their ages? Special needs at home, such as elderly parent and disabled family member? Career? Knowledge of the Faith?
3. Why are you seeking spiritual direction? (Professional ministry, discern a decision or experience, feeling lost or stuck in spiritual life, processing a trauma).
4. Tell me about your prayer life. Prayer routines.
5. What have you studied that has influenced your spiritual life? Who has inspired you in your spiritual life? (E.g. St. Ignatius of Loyola, *Theology of the Body*, Rosary, a parent's piety, a retreat, Charismatic Renewal, etc.)
6. What are you hoping to achieve through spiritual direction? (e.g. Accountability, learn new prayer techniques, make a decision, learn to listen to God, take seriously my call to discipleship, etc.).
7. Are you seeing any other professional counselors at this time? Should I be aware of any diagnosis or addiction at this time?
8. What is your current commitment to the Faith? Do you go to Mass? How often? Are you involved in any parish groups?
9. Explain confidentiality: Everything is held in confidence. The only time others would be involved is if the spiritual director is concerned that the person will harm himself or another person. As a mandatory reporter, the director is required to contact the authorities with information about child abuse.

10. (In the case of a person who needs to process trauma) Tell me about the trauma you experienced or are experiencing.
11. Affirm what you have heard thus far about the person, the reason they have come, and the situation they are in currently.
12. What are the achievable goals you aim to accomplish? (e.g. learn prayer techniques, discern a decision, learn about prayer and discernment, give the person a chance to process out loud their prayer experience, be accountable for a routine of prayer, begin to heal from trauma, etc.)
13. Parameters: How often will you meet? Any other requirements? (e.g. "I can only meet with you if you promise to... go to Mass, give up an addiction, etc.")
14. Ask the person to commit to three meetings. After three meetings, the person you are directing should be able to discern whether your style of direction is agreeable or not.
15. Set your first Plan of Action. (See handout).
16. Explain some basic terms: Discernment, Contemplation, Promptings of the Holy Spirit, Interior Movements, Virtue, etc.
17. Read or retell a suggested contemplation from the Plan of Action. The person you are directing may want to take notes.
18. Explain what an "Anchor Experience" is, and tell the person to be prepared to share an Anchor Experience at the next meeting.
19. Are there any questions?
20. Set the next meeting.
21. Let the other person guide the closing prayer.
22. Bless the person.

Spiritual Direction Sessions

1) Prior to this meeting, review the After Session Notes from the last meeting.
2) Begin by leading an opening prayer. Ask the Holy Spirit to guide you both.
3) How has your prayer life been since last time we met? Mass. Prayer Routine. Inner Movements.
4) Recap anything pertinent in your life since the last session.
5) Give a report of the last Plan of Action. Basically, give the directee a chance to summarize the journal entries.
6) Share an Anchor experience or any recent potential Promptings of the Holy Spirt.
7) (In the case of a person who needs to process trauma) Tell me about the trauma you experienced or are experiencing. Where are you with this? Have you been to counseling?
8) Affirm what you have heard thus far about the person, the reason they have come, and the situation they are in currently.
9) Give the next brief teaching about discernment of the Promptings of the Holy Spirit.
10) Are the established goals in need of revision?
11) (if this is the third meeting) Is your style of direction agreeable or would they like a recommendation for another director?
12) Set your next Plan of Action.
13) Read or retell a suggested contemplation from the Plan of Action. He/she may want to take notes.
14) Are there any questions?
15) Set next meeting

16) Let the other person guide the closing prayer.

17) Bless the person.

Notes of the Spiritual Director After a Session

Name of the Directed: ____________________

Date: ____________________

Phone #____________________

Email: ____

Name of Spouse (community): ____________________

Age of Children: ______________

1) Where in the Journey of Faith do you sense this person fits?

   Evangelization

   Spiritual

   Church Community

   Conversion

   Disciple

   Missionary

2) Are you aware of any spiritual gifts that the person manifests?
3) What virtue is the person trying to develop?
4) How attuned is the Spiritual Radar of this person to the promptings of the Holy Spirit?
5) What is the expressed reason for Spiritual Direction: Professional Ministry, Discernment, Lost/Stuck, Healing
6) What is the established goal for spiritual direction for this person?
7) What did you recommend him/her to study next?
8) What did you recommend him/her to contemplate?
9) How would you recommend adjusting his/her prayer routine?
10) What would be a good penance to recommend to reach the goals or progress in spiritual maturity?

Spiritual Plan of Action

Date: ______________________________

1) What is your established goal for Spiritual Direction?

2) Prayer Routine:

3) Suggested study: ________________________

4) Suggested biblical reading: ______________________

5) Suggested contemplative prayer:__________________________

6) For which grace will you petition the Lord? __________________

7) For next time, record in your journal:

    a. Insights from your
        i. Studies:
        ii. Assigned Contemplative Prayer:
        iii. Prayer Life:
    b. Did you experience any promptings of the Holy Spirit?
    c. Did you face any challenges or obstacles? How did you handle them?
    d. Did you have any notable temptations? How did you think through your response?
    e. Did you notice any virtues that you seem to possess? Are there any that seem underdeveloped?
    f. Any time you felt affirmed or had a reason to be grateful:
    g. How you prayed through any decisions and the results of those decisions.
    h. Did you have the opportunity to make amends for past mistakes?
    i. Any questions about faith that you might have had.

Stages of the Journey of Faith	Subset	Description	Identifying Attribute that a Person is Ready to Take the Next Step	Suggested Practice to Assist Progression to the Next Stage
Evangelization				
	Apathy	No interest in God, spirituality, or the Church	Begins to ask questions about faith	*Alpha* program. Come and See Weekend. Videos on Faith.
	Interest	Pays attention to conversations, friendships, and questions	Can articulate a personal, though undeveloped, faith	*Alpha* program. *Come and See* Weekend. Speeches. Apologetics (atheism, science and religion).
	Belief	Recognizes God/ Jesus/ Spirit as being important	Speaks of a desire to know the living Christ	Encountering Christ Retreat.
Spiritual				
	Encounter with Christ	Has mystical, personal experience of Jesus. Feels the fire of Christ's presence and love	Wants be identified with Christ	Read Sacred Scripture or derivative writings. Apologetics (Christianity).
	Trust Christ	Accepts that Jesus is the answer to life's questions	Wants to be identified with parish	Apologetics (religion). Invitation to spiritual and catechetical events at the parish. Reading the history of the Church. Pilgrimage.
	Discipline of Prayer	Prays, even alone. Expresses a love of Christ and acknowledges Christ's love.	Realizes God has expectations of us.	Conversion Retreat. Reflections on the Cross and Salvation.
Conversion				
	Moral Awakening	Realizes right from wrong beyond the universal norms	Wants to be a "good" person who pleases the Lord.	Examination of Conscious. Sacrament of Reconciliation. Reflections on the lives of the Saints. Pilgrimage.
	Conversion	Wants to change his or her life.	Takes serious the change in their life decisions and use of time. Is repentant of sins.	Moral teachings explained. Spiritual Direction.

Page 2

Stages of the Journey of Faith	Subset	Description	Identifying Attribute that a Person is Ready to Take the Next Step	Suggested Practice to Assist Progression to the Next Stage
	Metanoia of Life	Calculates all the changes of life required to stay consistent with the conversion experience.	Willing to volunteer.	*Come and See* Weekend. Ministry Fair. Role models of living the faith. *Joyfully Gifted* program. Experience of charity and service in the name of the Church.
Discipleship				
	Commitment	Willing to devote time and energy to a ministry of interest.	Asks what God wants of them.	Spiritual Direction. Spiritual Principles. Charismatic Movement. Discernment Retreat. Reading a spiritual book.
	Spirit-Guided	Allows the Holy Spirit to direct the decisions of how to use time, energy, and resources	Is interested in and prays for the needs of others they do not even know personally.	Articles about efforts of the diocese or the global Church. Mission Trip. Assisting works of charity. Experience a variety of ministries.
Missionary				
	Catholic Vision	Becomes aware of the needs of those outside the usual circle of interest	Begins to see specific remedies to systematic problems in the Church and society.	Read contemporary news articles. Group discussions about modern topics. Appreciate historical responses to past crises. Dialogue with authorities.
	Prophetic Role	Realizes God's work and our role in shaping society	Listens to someone else tell their journey of faith without simply applying to his or her own decisions. Desire to start new groups.	Envision what can be accomplished. Envision those who have needs, but are not being cared for. Dialogue with authorities.
	Leadership	Leads others, within the context of the Church and the promptings of the Holy Spirit		

Suggested Penances for Building Up Virtues

Virtue	Penance
Generosity	Enjoy a day without spending money. Give of your time by visiting a nursing home or a hospital. Simplify your wardrobe or the clutter in your house without replacing it all with new things. Dedicate a little extra time helping a family member with their tasks.
Humility	Listen to someone else without drawing attention to yourself. Realize how often people must tolerate you. Do some menial work that does not require your skills while not seeking approval. Do some anonymous charitable work in the name of someone else. Meet with your family and let them remind you of the funny mistakes you made as a child. Recall a time that someone misjudged you and realize you may have done the same to others. Is there anyone you need to ask for forgiveness or make amends with?

Chastity	Fast. Study *Theology of the Body.* Be honest with a trusted friend to have an intimate, non-romantic experience. If you are not greatly tempted, learn about or comfort a victim of sexual abuse. Disconnect access to the internet during your most tempted hours in such a way that it would take considerable effort to re-connect it. Do something especially loving, though non-physical, for your spouse.
Honesty	Contemplate Jesus with Pilate. Contemplate the courage of a soldier, able to face the consequences of war. Contemplate the importance of having someone believe you when you tell them about Christ, salvation, the moral life, etc. Quickly admit when you exaggerated or lied, even though it is embarrassing. Practice the Three-Second Rule.
Reverence	Clean or decorate the church or some part of it. Give praise to God with various expressions. Write a personal prayer. Tell someone about your admiration for the glory of God.

	Contemplate the hope of salvation and the terror of condemnation with gratitude for Christ. Marvel at creation.
Diligence	Clean your office or your house or some part of it. Do manual labor. Create a task list. Admire a diligent person. Reward yourself for accomplishing a task. Give thanks to God for accomplishing a task by an act of reverence.
Discipline	Wake up at 3:00 AM for prayers before returning to sleep. Form and stick to a prayer routine. Use the Ignatian *Examen* to help you focus on improving. Ask a friend to help keep you accountable. Admit your failings quickly with the firm resolve to do better. Cut out television and internet for a time.
Charity	Do an activity with someone else that you do not particularly enjoy. Do an act of charity or service. Make it a point to greet three people you do not typically greet. Look for the "outcasts" of any group and make it a point to include them.

	Is there anyone you need to forgive?
Patience	Pray before the Blessed Sacrament for an hour. Use the Ignatian *Examen* to prepare for the occasions that usually test your patience. Let someone tell a story you have already heard. Accompany someone in a waiting room.
Courage	Contemplate the courage of the Saints. Contemplate the rewards of heaven. Contemplate the consolation of the Sacred Heart of Jesus. Contemplate the intercession of the Army of Saints. Contemplate walking the road of life with Christ. Contemplate the brevity of our suffering and the eternity of our proudly telling Christ what we have done for His Sake.
Gratitude	List your blessings. Tell someone how much you appreciate them. Contemplate those who suffer poverty. Contemplating the complimentary nature of gifts that you have and do not have with respect to other members of the community.

	Contemplate the many ways God might have provided for you without your knowledge. Thank God for the blessings you do not have because they probably would have corrupted you. Do an act of reverence to show your gratitude for something specific (e.g. visit a shrine).
Temperance	Fast. Eat and drink more simple/ less flavorful food, so as to satisfy hunger while being free from the attachment to flavor. Give up, for a time, a creature comfort without letting anyone know of your sacrifice. Contemplate the possible scenario where you may have to heroically resist your worldly desires for the sake of God's greater desire.
Forgiveness	Contemplate how the Virgin Mary had no room in her heart for hatred. Realize how much you have been forgiven. Work toward healing. Contemplate the protection of your dignity by the Truth of Christ.

Obedience	Joyfully accept an inferior decision. Let someone else make a decision. Share your authority with someone else. Offer a compliment to a decision someone else made. Actively seek to understand the perspective of an authority or of someone you have authority over. Contemplate the immaturity of a teenager who rebelliously ignores good advice.
Tolerance	Consider all the people who, unbeknownst to you, are tolerant of you. Contemplate the parable of the Wheat and the Weeds. Contemplate a tired mother rocking a crying baby. Contemplate the grey area that none of us are completely good or bad. Contemplate what it means to "love your enemies." Think of the moment of struggling to tolerate someone as similar to a physical exercise where you are increasing your endurance.

Glossary

A

Accompaniment – a term from Pope Francis; walking with people on their faith journey without pressuring or judging them. The goal is less about trying to convert a person or give them advice or answers and more about giving the person the space and opportunity to reflect on the meaning and importance of spirituality.

Accountability – one of the main goals of spiritual direction; keeping people honest about maintaining their discipline of prayer and practice of virtue.

Agony in the Garden – a prayer technique designed to help us experience the weight of the Sacred Heart; involves imagining yourself in the Garden of Gethsemane with the Lord.

Anchor Experience – a key moment in your life when you are most confident that God communicated with you. This moment can be used in the discernment of the authenticity of God's communication in new moments of mystical experiences.

Angel of Light – a term from St. Ignatius; the devil disguises himself as a good angel in order to lead us astray. The individual person is incapable of seeing that this prompting is not from God while others can see it clearly. This points to the importance of discerning with others.

Angels – God's messengers; created by God and used by Him as a means of intervening in human history; very little is known about them.

Anger – the sin of revenge, resentment, passive-aggressive behavior, violence, verbal abuse, unforgiveness, slander, and wishing harm on someone.

Anonymous Intervention – God intervenes in our lives to help us without our knowledge of the divine activity.

Attachments (1) – spiritual warfare term; feelings of a connection to some belief or influence that is not of God; combat this with routine prayer to help reorient the mind and heart toward the things of God.

Attachments (2) – excessive attachment to or unhealthy dependence on material goods or people; temptation to greed.

B

Be Mindful of the Listener – the skill of being aware of how you say something and how the listener will receive it and speaking accordingly in order to best serve the listener.

Bite-Sized Pieces – set small, achievable goals in the spiritual life so as not to get overwhelmed with the thought of how much we must change to be holy.

Blessed – a title for a person moving forward in the canonization process, but who is not yet officially recognized as an official Saint.

Broken Vocations – the tragic sense that your vocation was thwarted, incomplete, or unrealized; people must find healing in order to reenter a trusting relationship with God.

C

Celibacy – a discipline of the Church to not enter into marriage or a romantic relationship; provides freedom to be solely focused on and fully committed to the Mission of the Church and the promptings of the Holy Spirit.

Charity – the virtue opposed to anger; involves seeking the good of others, forgiveness, resolving conflict out of love rather than dominance, and taking the time to heal deeper wounds.

Chastity – the virtue opposed to lust; proper respect for others as persons and not as objects for sexual entertainment; a proper understanding the dignity and value of attraction and sexuality.

Church Community Stage - the third stage of the Journey of Faith; people begin to look to the Church for answers to their questions, begin to attend a parish regularly, and begin to develop a personal prayer life.

Church Tradition – the wealth of knowledge from Church teaching, the writings of the Saints, and oral traditions that we can draw upon for spiritual advice and proper interpretation of the Sacred Scriptures and of the Catholic Faith.

Community – one reason for the Sunday Obligation; we are members of the People of God, not merely individuals; this spirituality should inspire us and lead us to work together for the sake of the Gospel.

Companion for the Journey – the role of a spiritual director; meant to help interpret and encourage the spiritual life of those they direct.

Competing Athletes – just as athletes make sacrifices and work daily toward their goals, we too must constantly strive for perfection in the spiritual life, going above and beyond the standards of our culture.

Conflict – rooted in 1) an injustice that needs healing, 2) a confusion that needs clarification, or 3) opposing paradigms of thinking and methods of reaching goals; always remember to goal of the conflict and only enter into conflicts out of love.

Conscience – used to determine right and wrong; must be properly formed through study and training.

Contemplate Heaven – a prayer exercise that involves imagining what Heaven will be like in order to increase our desire for it.

Contemplation – a form of prayer meant to help us ponder the mysteries of the Faith.

Counseling – distinct from spiritual direction; looks for the root causes of issues and corrects them; primarily concerned with the way past experiences influences the perspective of current events, whereas spiritual direction considers the interpretation of life from the perspective of Faith.

Conversion Stage – the fourth stage of the Journey of Faith; people have an awakening to the moral law of love; they change their lives to become better disciples and to reject sin.

Cross Verify – discernment method involving comparing a private revelation to the Deposit of Faith; God does not change, so if a private revelation is inconsistent with the Deposit of Faith, it is not from God.

D

Defensiveness – a spiritual danger in conflicts; occurs when a person is so attached to his opinion to the point that he takes a rejection of the opinion as a personal rejection, leading him to engage in personal attacks, isolating the opponent, or avoiding the issue; defensiveness is based in pride, not in love.

Deliverance Ministry – ministry aimed at gaining spiritual freedom; focuses on removing "cancerous" negative emotions that enslave us.

Demons – fallen angels who tempt us; they can influence humans or objects, but Christ is always more powerful than they are; information about them is shrouded in lies, making it difficult to know their true nature.

Deposit of Faith – collection of Divine Revelation handed down through the centuries and guarded by the Catholic Church; composed of Sacred Scripture and the Catholic Tradition.

Diligence – the virtue opposed to sloth; being responsible and fulfilling your duties.

Discernment – the process of recognizing Divine communication and making decisions with the Lord based on His preference.

Disciple Stage – the fifth stage of the Journey of Faith; people commit their time to serve the Lord, devote energy toward ministry, and learn how to let the Holy Spirit direct them.

Discipline – sacrificing our immediate desires for the sake of our duty.

Disillusionment – the temptation to dismiss the Church as corrupt or unholy based upon the sins and scandals of Church members.

Divine Providence – God's Divine Plan unfolding in time; God has a purpose for everything; we are called to participate in His Plan.

Do Not Test the Lord – a warning not to try to make deals with God regarding our behavior, which is insulting to God; we cannot force God to do anything or call Him unfaithful if He does not do what we want. Nor are we to attempt to make God prove His existence or goodness according to our own criteria.

Dream Interpretation – while God can use dream to communicate, it is often the subjective meaning of the dream to the dreamer that matters more than the dream itself.

E

Ego – the second of the Four Voices; you mentally "speaking" to yourself; encompasses your thoughts, desires, hopes, and worries; not bad, just not God. It is the self in the thinking process.

Emotionalism – seeking positive emotions to the detriment of your relationship with God; chasing after feelings, rather than pursuing God.

Envy – the sin of desiring the blessings of others or wishing that others did not have such blessings.

Escapism – using distractions to ignore our duties and the stress they cause; in the spiritual life, this is using prayer to avoid our responsibilities by claiming all our worries are in God's hands.

Evangelization Stage – the first stage of the Journey of Faith; people progress from being apathetic about faith, to being interested, to believing that there is truth in faith; no commitment.

Examen – a prayer method from St. Ignatius of Loyola; pray in the morning, midday, and evening, examining your day each time; meant to help you prepare to exercise virtue and improve your consistency in virtue by praying and self-evaluating throughout the day.

F

Fear of the Lord – the virtue of giving God the respect and reverence He deserves.

Fidelity to Church Teaching – a promise made by theologians, catechists and those holding an official office of the Church, such as pastor or parochial vicar; knowing, understanding, and promoting Church teaching; giving proper reverence to the teaching authority of the Church.

Field Hospital – an image for the Church from Pope Francis: the Church is a hospital for sick souls; the Church members aim is not to isolate themselves from sinners, but to engage the sinners in an attempt to bring them spiritual health.

Final Judgment – based upon the decisions of our lives, the Lord decides if we spend our eternal life in either Heaven or Hell; our actions in our daily lives matter to God and to our immortal lives.

Find the Patterns – a method of discernment used to 1) notice a Divine Plan unfolding so we can better participate in it or 2) recognize the sins we consistently commit so we can better defend against those specific temptations; requires caution so as not to imagine a pattern that is not truly there.

Fire Alarms – powerful emotions that indicate a deeper reality; meant to illustrate our need to respond to the reality that causes emotional reactions rather than to merely respond to the emotion, itself.

Force Fit – the opposite of Holy Indifference and Discernment; attempting to interpret God's communication to agree with our desires.

Four Reasons – people might seek spiritual direction because 1) they are in the pastoral care of others, 2) they are trying to make a significant decision, 3) they feel spiritually lost or stuck, or 4) they are processing a traumatic experience.

Four Voices – a discernment technique used to distinguish the voices of God, the Ego, the Projected Voice, and the Tempter within the interior conversation of one's own mind.

Free Will – humanity's ability to choose to cooperate with or to resist the Divine Plan; a prerequisite for the ability to love.

G

Generosity – the virtue opposed to greed; involves appropriate desires for material goods and a willingness to share your resources with others.

Ghosts – very little is known about them; could exist spiritually or only in the mind.

Gift of Healing – the gift of healing people through prayer by the power of the Holy Spirit; can be physical or spiritual healing. It is not a power that is under the direct control of the person; authority for its use continues to depend on the Holy Spirit.

Gift of Interpretation of Tongues – the gift of being able to understand and interpret the words of someone who has the charismatic gift of speaking in tongues.

Gift of Tongues – the gift of praying freely in another language or in pre-lingual gibberish; oftentimes, the person does not know what he is saying, but simply allows the Holy Spirit to pray through him or her.

Gift of Words of Knowledge – the gift of sensing a message from God intended for a person in the group or the whole group over whom you are praying.

Gluttony – the sin of excess; traditionally, it is an excess of food or drink, but it can apply to many other things, such as television or internet.

God Does Not Micromanage – the spiritual principle that God calls us to actively participate in His Divine Plan, but He allows us to make decisions of our own within that Plan without controlling us or limiting our creativity.

God is Gentle – the spiritual principle that God is gentle with us so as not to overwhelm us, who are small and fragile in comparison to Him; God gently indicates what He wants, but He never forces us to act.

God is Greater Than I Can Imagine – the spiritual principle that we cannot fully understand God because He is so much greater than can be conceived by our limited minds. We can know God, while never exhausting all there is to know about God.

God's Timing – God knows exactly when to intervene and when not to intervene in order to fulfill His Plan; we must trust God's timing.

God's Veto Power – if we are open to the Holy Spirit and give Him permission, He can veto our decisions when necessary and guide us to a better path

God Will Not Be Mocked – saying in words that we want to be with Christ for all eternity is not enough if our actions say we do not want this; it is mocking God to say you want to be with Him while living as though you have no interest in Heaven. See Galatians 6:7.

Grateful for My Failures – we should be grateful that our failures can 1) inadvertently serve the Divine Plan, 2) help us become more self-aware and thus better prepared to resist temptations and mistaken tendencies, 3) remind us of our need for a Savior.

Gratitude – the virtue opposed to the vice of envy; being aware of and appreciating the blessings you have; being happy for others when they receive blessings. Loving the Gift-Giver more than the gift.

Greed – the sin involving a disordered desire for more material goods, an excessive fear of losing what you have, a disordered desire to identify one's worth or relative worth compared to others based on material possessions, or an unwillingness to share your resources.

Grieve the Dead – Christ gave us permission to grieve when He cried at the death of Lazarus; our sadness indicates that we miss the dead, not that we doubt God's mercy.

H

Heavenly Makeover – an analogy for Purgatory; the process of preparing a soul to enter Heaven; some of this process happens here on Earth, but, if people die before it is complete, it can be finished in Purgatory.

Hell – the place of eternal punishment for those who choose to be separate from God.

Holy Indifference – detachment from any specific outcome; placing God's Will above your own so that you are willing to accept any decision from God even if it differs from your desire.

Honesty – the virtue of speaking the truth even when it is difficult or will does not lead to one's own preference; a protection against the lies and confusion that veils one's perception.

Humility – the virtue opposed to pride; being accepting of yourself as you are without the need to change the perceptions of others to see you as you wish you were; placing the needs of others before your own.

I

Immortality Pill – a thought exercise about what would happen if we invented a pill that would prevent us from dying; leads to the conclusion that the hope of Heaven is what makes our lives meaningful and that a life lived forever on Earth is not as good as life lived forever in Heaven.

Intercessory Prayer – the act of praying for another person; we do not fully understand how this works, but we know from Scripture and Tradition that it does make a difference.

Internal Movements – a concept from St. Ignatius of Loyola; the emotions and reactions to a Divine message; can be indicators of God's Will according to our understanding that God knows what emotions His communication will evoke.

Involuntary Thoughts – thoughts that pop into your mind without your choosing; not sinful because there is no freedom involved; simply recognize them and move on.

J

Jesus Before Pontius Pilate – a prayer exercise intended to help you grow in honesty; contemplate Jesus' refusal to lie despite the consequences.

Journaling – a form of prayer with two main benefits: 1) it forces you to slow down and 2) it helps you organize your thoughts.

Journey of Faith – the six non-chronological stages people go through when growing in faith and in relationship with the Lord; 1) Evangelization 2) Spiritual Awakening 3) Church Community 4) Conversion 5) Disciple 6) Missionary.

K

Kisses from Heaven – little blessings from God sent as reminders of His love and affection for us. They may not be necessary to change decisions and outcomes but they please the Lord to be affectionate.

L

Let the Holy Spirit Drive – putting God and the Divine Plan above our own hopes, dreams, desires, and plans, trusting Him to make better decisions than we ever could.

Life of Prayer – a vow/promise made by priests and religious and, to a lesser extent, by all the baptized; this commitment to prayer nurtures a relationship with God and a sense of self in relation to God.

Looking to the Fruits – a retrospective method of discernment from St. Paul's Letter to the Galatians; involves analyzing past decisions and what the results of those decisions were; if the decision was truly from God, it will result in the Fruits of the Spirit.

Lowest Common Denominator – the most outrageous of sinners; we compare ourselves to this sinner in order to comfort ourselves and justify our own sinfulness. A way of valuing ourselves by being comparatively better than some.

Lust – the sin of using sex and sexual attraction solely for the purpose of pleasure; reducing people to objects for sexual entertainment; includes pornography, masturbation, fornication, adultery, sexual fantasies, sexual abuse, etc.

M

Magic – the attempt to manipulate people, objects, luck, or historical events through spiritual practices; should be completely avoided; prayer is not magic.

Married Couples – vow to be faithful (chastity and monogamy), to love and respect each other, and to be open to having children; must have the utmost concern for the salvation of their spouse.

Megachurches – large, Evangelical churches that cover huge territories and usually depend on a charismatic personality; may be a source of envy for Catholics; may be part of God's plan to slowly draw people to a healthier, more evangelizing Catholic Church.

Mind of Christ – an application of Prayerful Imagination; involves imagining ourselves, others, and the world the way Christ sees us.

Ministry of Mercy – recognition that all people are both good and bad at different times, leading to pity for sinners and a desire for their repentance, conversion, and salvation.

Minor Rite of Exorcism – an optional, but recommended, prayer in the baptismal ritual; asks for God's protection over the baptized.

Missionary Stage – the sixth stage of the Journey of Faith; guided by the Holy Spirit, people consider the Catholic Vision, the Prophetic Role, and the Call to Leadership; they take seriously the needs of people outside their normal circles, recognize their efforts as part of God's work, and coordinate with others to further a common goal.

Moderation – see *Temperence*.

Mortal Sin – a sin 1) involving a serious matter, 2) committed with full knowledge of the sinfulness of the act, and 3) committed freely.

Mystery – a being or idea that can be known to a certain extent, but never fully known.

O

Obedience – a vow or promise made by priests and religious; this requires submitting one's opinion and will to a superior, trusting that his or her authority over you and the unity of decision making serves the will of God.

Obsession – incessant thoughts that are contrary to God or to the reality that God has revealed; combat this with deliverance prayers and, in some cases, a professional counselor or trained priest.

Occult – practices such as Ouija boards, fortune tellers, séances, magic spells, pagan rituals, or curses; explicitly forbidden in the Old Testament and in the writings of St. Paul; dangerous because they invite ungodly forces into our lives and because they warp our way of thinking about God, ourselves, and prayer.

Old Self – a Pauline illustration of the sinful way we lived and thought before we committed to Christ and took seriously the conversion process.

Old Sins Remembered – a person is bothered by thoughts of a sin that has already been forgiven; could involve an unhealed wound related to the sin, a tendency toward that sin, or a belief that he is unworthy of God's mercy.

Oppression – a more intense spiritual attack; a person's obsessive thoughts begin to interrupt his daily life and prevent him from seeking help; healing requires the work of professionals and should not be attempted by a regular spiritual director alone.

Other-Centered – a spirituality based on being less concerned with yourself and more concerned about your neighbor; emphasizes the importance of community.

P

Parish Priests – their role is to come to know the members of their congregation, discern the spiritual needs of the congregation, be creative in addressing those spiritual needs, and work in collaboration with the gifts of the people both inside and outside of the parish, sacrificing for the good of the parish when necessary.

Pastoral Care – the first reason someone might seek spiritual direction; a field of professional ministers whom others seek for guidance.

Patience – the virtue of responding calmly and respectfully to stressful situations, annoying personalities, or accompanying someone who is gradually coming to the right conclusion without hurrying the process.

Pelagian Heresy – the false view that we must earn Heaven; in reality, we cannot get to Heaven on our own, so we need a Savior.

Penances – part of Virtue Building; spiritual practices designed to develop virtue or overcome a tendency toward vice.

Pick Your Battles – being prudent about which conflicts to engage in and which to let go; only enter into conflict out of love for the other and when the issue is worth fighting for.

Possession – a person begins to lose his identity and becomes resistant to any form of treatment; in some cases, a person may experience more extreme manifestations; the diagnosis and treatment of a possession should never be undertaken by an average spiritual director; the diocesan exorcist should be contacted if there is suspicion of a possession.

Prayer of St. Thérèse, the Little Flower – say twenty-four Glory Be's each day for twenty-four days; if you receive a rose during these twenty-four days, it is a sign that your prayer was granted; if you do not receive a rose, it is a sign that the answer was no or that God has chosen not to tell you the answer.

Prayer for the Dead – a form of intercessory prayer; we do not fully understand how it works, but Scripture and Tradition tell us that we ought to pray for the dead; our prayers can assist those in Purgatory on their journey, or cleansing process, toward Heaven.

Prayerful Imagination – using our God-given imaginations to help us better envision the Mysteries of the Faith, allowing the Holy Spirit to guide our minds to a deeper understanding and faith.

Pre-Lingual Communication – communicating on a deep level that resonates more with our humanity than our learned vocabulary; communicating without words.

Presenting My Worries – a prayer exercise involving naming our worries and placing them in a basket to give to Jesus, then praying without the weight of our worries, then accepting back only those worries Jesus wants us to take back up and leaving the rest with Him.

Presume God's Mercy – the sin of assuming that, because we have a Savior, we are permitted to continue sinning and do not need to make a sincere effort to stop sinning and begin living holy lives.

Priest From India – a mental exercise designed to help find motivation to pray; imagine a priest from India who is also struggling to finish his prayers; by trying to motivate him to stay faithful, you will also be motivated to pray for the sake of duty and to encourage this priest.

Pride – the sin of being self-centered, selfish, inconsiderate, judgmental, considering yourself superior (or inferior) to others, vanity, false humility, or looking for honors, adoration, attention, or unearned respect.

Private Revelation – communication from God to individuals; a revelation to a person which is in line with the Deposit of Faith and adds nothing new to it; meant for that individual or his circle of influence.

Projected Voice – the third of the Four Voices; includes the voices, thoughts, and opinions of all the people who have influenced us, especially role models; not bad, just not God; it is good to be inspired by others, so long as we recognize that this voice is not God.

Promptings by the Holy Spirit – various forms of Divine Communication, such as words, themes, or feelings; must be interpreted properly to find the meaning that will lead us closer to God.

Purgatory – a place of purification to make souls ready for Heaven; these souls have already chosen God, but they need further preparation before they can enter Heaven.

Purgatory Pool – a spiritual concept involving all those whom you find difficult to love; we must make peace and/or amends with these people before we can enter Heaven; we can begin this process here on Earth.

Purifying Your Prayer – a technique used when we are frustrated with prayer; under each prayer, there is a deeper desire; Christ may not give us what we ask for, but He will satisfy the desire underneath the prayer.

Put Words into God's Mouth – a common error in discernment; occurs when we misattribute certain messages to God so that we hear what we want to hear from Him.

R

Reciprocal Grace – the reward for doing good works; "And your Father who sees what is hidden will repay you." (Matthew 6:18). The positive feelings or benefits from doing what is good and holy.

Revelation – information about God that we could not discover on our own, so we needed God to reveal it to us.

Reverence – the virtue of appropriate respect for God and for holy people, places, and objects; involves being disciplined in prayer, deliberately participating in ritual, and paying special attention and respect to people committed to the spiritual life.

Rituals – a ceremony or specified action that is repeated regularly; reach to the universal human experience and shape our lives.

S

Sacrament of Baptism – the normative way in which we accept Christ's gift of grace, become members of the Church, are identified as God's adopted children, and forgiven from both personal and original sin; ritual of having water poured on the head with the words: "I baptize you in the Name of the Father, and of the Son, and of the Holy Spirit."

Sacred Heart of Jesus – heavy with the sin and suffering of the world; we bring comfort to Jesus when we desire to know and carry His burden.

Sacrifice – offered as a prayer in imitation of our Lord on the Cross and united with His suffering; can be an act of gratitude of an expression of our love for God

Saints – a person who is officially declared to be in Heaven and worthy of imitation and intercession. The Saint is officially canonized by the Church after a long process of studying the person's life and miracles attributed to them.

Salt Water – an image used to describe the ill-effects of pornography; pornography is like salt water: you think it will satisfy your thirst, but it will only make you thirstier and eventually make you sick.

Sanctifying the Memory – a prayer exercise designed to help people process traumatic memories; involves remembering and describing the traumatic event and looking for Christ in the memory; if you cannot find Christ, imagine watching the same event through a camera, as though you are outside of the event, and look for Christ again; speak to Him and let Him remind you that you are not alone.

Scapegoat Mechanism – a term from René Girard; a weapon of the devil; as a group, we arbitrarily choose someone to blame for societal issues and punish him in some way to make ourselves feel better without addressing the underlying issues.

Search for Potential Saints – a prayer technique involving an awareness of those in our lives who are also seeking to be saints so that we can motivate and help each other.

Second Copy of the Ten Commandments – a story from Exodus 32-34 that demonstrates the power of intercessory prayer.

Serenity Prayer – "Lord, grant me the serenity to accept the things I cannot change, the courage to change the things I can, and the wisdom to know the difference. Amen."

Shepherd – Christ is our Shepherd; if we know Him, we will be able to recognize His voice.

Significant Decision – the second reason someone might seek spiritual direction; this usually occurs during a significant transitional phase or a difficult decision-making process.

Silence – a form of prayer with no words; resting and being quiet with the Lord.

Single Life – one of the vocations; sometimes viewed with stigma, but perfectly valid despite this.

Slain in the Spirit – a Charismatic experience; occurs when one person prays over another and the individual who was prayed over falls over, becoming semi-conscious in total submission of mind and body to the Holy Spirit; afterwards, many feel joy, a release of stress, or other blessings or freedoms.

Sloth – sins of omission in our duties; not being proactive in initiating projects or helping others.

Spiritual Awakening Stage – the second stage of the Journey of Faith; people have an encounter with the Lord, leading to trust in Him; Christ becomes an active Person in their lives, rather than just a thought or a historical figure.

Spiritual, but Not Religious – an individual who claims to be holy, pray, and follow God without any organized religion or objective standards or rules.

Spiritual Radar – a constant awareness of how God is communicating with you in your daily life.

Spiritually Lost – the third reason someone might seek spiritual direction; this occurs when people are struggling spiritually and need help to strengthen their faith

Stewardship – see *Generosity.*

Suicide – murder and grave matter; can be a mortal sin if it meets the three criteria, but can also be a grave venial sin if the individual's culpability is reduced by mental illness.

T

Temperence – the virtue opposed to gluttony; consuming goods only as much as we need to be satisfied, without slipping into excess; recognizing that living a holy life is greater than feeding the desires of the body.

Temptation –a way of thinking about and evaluating options and the desired outcomes of those options that is not in line with God's Will.

Three-Second Rule – used to develop honesty; when you feel pressured and want to lie, mentally count to three before speaking; helps calm the impulse to lie.

Tolerance – the ability to remain calm and humble in the face of the temptation to be angry with a perceived injustice or annoyance.

Traumatic Experience – the fourth reason someone might seek spiritual direction; this occurs when a person's past affects how he sees God, others, and himself in a negative way; he needs healing from his trauma in order to mend his relationship with God; the individual should seek professional counseling in addition to spiritual direction.

U

Unconditional Love – willing the good of the other consistently, regardless of how he makes you feel or what he can do for you; love that is not based upon an attribute of the other, but based upon his person.

Universal Call to Holiness – all people are called to be holy and imitate Christ; we should all desire to be saints.

Universal Salvation – the concept that the gift of Salvation is not exclusive, but is offered to all people; each person can choose to accept or reject this gift.

Unveiling the Mask – the spiritual practice of showing our Lord who we really are, rather than the mask we present to the world; allowing our Lord to love us as we are and not as who we pretend to be.

V

Venial Sin – sin that is 1) not of grave matter, 2) committed out of ignorance, or 3) not committed freely.

Virtue Building – a method of spiritual growth; name a particular sin you want to overcome; name the opposite virtue; develop penances to help you grow in that virtue.

Vocation – a calling to 1) single life, 2) married life, 3) religious life, or 4) priesthood; spiritual direction is a helpful tool for discerning a vocation; must be a free choice, a full commitment, and intended to be a lifelong commitment.

Voice of God – the first of the Four Voices; the voice we want to verify using the Four Voices method.

Voice of the Tempter – the fourth of the Four Voices; the devil tempts us to sin to keep us away from the Divine Plan; any thoughts from the Tempter should be immediately shut down; we should name our temptations in order to better defend against them and remind us of our need for a Savior, but we should never dialogue with the Tempter.

Voluntary Thoughts – thoughts we intentionally dwell on or fantasize about; can be sinful because they require a free choice.

Vow of Poverty – a promise made by some religious communities; intended to encourage a spirituality of solidarity with the poor, simplicity of life, and dependence on God.

W

Wartime Radio – an analogy for prayer; as with a radio, we must carefully seek a signal in prayer; the brief messages we receive motivate and direct us in continuing our spiritual fight.

Without My Eyes – a true story depicting how little we know about what Heaven will actually be like.

Words of Prophecy – a message from God to a person or a group in a thought or a vision; usually a call to prayer, confidence in the Lord, or a recognition that the Lord knows what we are going through.

Worst Sin – a logical sequence to demonstrate the power of God's mercy; starts with lesser sins, eventually progressing to the worst sin: torturing and killing the only Son of God; if God can forgive even this worst sin, surely, He can forgive any sin.

Worth Even More – the principle that if we do not want to go to Mass but still go out of a sense of obligation and love for God, it is "worth even more".

Bibliography

Aquinas, Thomas. *Summa Theologiae Prima Pars, 50-119*. Translated by Laurence Shapcote. Edited by The Aquinas Institute. Green Bay, WI: Aquinas Institute, Inc., 2018.

Beckman, Kathleen. *A Family Guide to Spiritual Warfare: Strategies for Deliverance and Healing*. Manchester, NH: Sophia Institute Press, 2020.

Benedict XVI. "Deus Caritas Est." December 25, 2005. https://vatican.va/content/benedict-xvi/en/encyclicals/documents/hf_ben-xvi_enc_20051225_deus-caritas-est.html.

Butler, Alban. *Butler's Lives of the Saints: Complete Edition*, Vol. 1. Edited by Herbert Thurston and Donald Attwater. Westminster, MD: Christian Classics, Inc., 1956.

Catechism of the Catholic Church, Second Edition. Washington, DC: United States Conference of Catholic Bishops, 2019.

Churchill, Winston. *Winston S. Churchill: His Complete Speeches 1897-1963*. Edited by Robert Rhodes James. New York, NY: Chelsea House Publishers, 1974.

de Voragine, Jacobus. *The Golden Legend*. Translated by William Caxton. Edited by George V. O'Neill. London: Cambridge University Press, 1914.

Descartes, René. *A Discourse on Method*. Translated by John Veitch. London: J. M. Dent & Sons LTD, 1975.

Drake, Bruce. "Number of Christians Rises, but Their Share of World Population Stays Stable." Pew Research Center, March 22, 2013. https://www.pewresearch.org/short-reads/2013/03/

22/number-of-christians-rises-but-their-share-of-world-population-stays-stable/#:~:text=There%20are%202.18%20billion%20Christians,Forum%20on%20Religion%20%26%20Public%20Life.

Fatima in Lucia's Own Words: Sister Lucia's Memoirs. Edited by Louis Kondor. Translated by Dominican Nuns of Perpetual Rosary. Cambridge, MA: Ravengate Press, 1976.

Francis. "General Audience of 28 August 2019." General Audience of 28 August 2019 | Francis, August 28, 2019. https://www.vatican.va/content/francesco/en/audiences/2019/documents/papa-francesco_20190828_udienza-generale.html.

Hampton Wright, Vinita. "Finding God in Our Desires." Ignatian Spirituality, July 13, 2023. https://ignatianspirituality.com/finding-god-in-our-desires/.

Ignatius of Loyola. *The Autobiography of St. Ignatius of Loyola*. Edited by John C. Olin. Translated by Joseph F. O'Callaghan. New York: Harper & Row, Publishers, Inc., 1974.

Ignatius of Loyola, *The Text of the Spiritual Exercises of Saint Ignatius*. London: Burns and Oates, Limited, 1900.

Ivens, Michael. *Understanding the Spiritual Exercises: A Handbook for Retreat Directors*. Leominster, England: Gracewing, 1998.

John of the Cross. *John of the Cross: Selected Writings*. Edited and Translated by Kieran Kavanaugh. Mahwah, NJ: Paulist Press, 1987.

Kirby, Jeffrey. *The Life and Witness of Saint Maria Goretti: Our Little Saint of the Beatitudes*. Charlottle, NC: TAN Books, 2015.

Kraljevic, Svetozar. *The Apparitions of Our Lady at Medjugorje 1981-1983: An Historical Account with Interviews.* Edited by Michael Scanlan. Chicago, IL: Franciscan Herald Press, 1984.

Lewis, C.S., Mere Christianity. New York: Macmillan Publishing Co., Inc., 1952.

Lorit, Sergius C. *The Last Days of Maximilian Kolbe.* Brooklyn, NY: New City Press, 1982.

Lozano, Neal. *Unbound.* United States of America: Chosen Books, 2010.

Marx, Groucho. *Groucho and Me.* New York: Bernard Geis Associates, 1959.

McFerrin, Bobby. *Simple Pleasures.* Capitol Records, 1988.

Merton, Thomas. *Thoughts in Solitude.* New York: Farrar, Straus & Cudahy, 1958.

Mother Teresa, *Mother Teresa: Come Be My Light: The Private Writings of the "Saint of Calcutta."* Edited by Brian Kolodiejchuk. New York: Doubleday, 2007.

O'Brien, Kevin. *The Ignatius Adventure: Experiencing the Spiritual Exercises of Saint Ignatius in Daily Life.* Chicago: Loyola Press, 2011.

Paul VI. "Dei Verbum." Dogmatic Constitution on Divine Revelation: Dei Verbum, November 18, 1965. https://vatican.va/archive/hist_councils/ii_vatican_council/documents/vat-ii_const_19651118_dei-verbum_en.html.

Therese of Lisieux, *Story of a Soul: The Autobiography of St. Therese of Lisieux.* Translated by John Clarke. Washington, D.C.: Institute of Carmelite Studies Publications, 1976.

"The Twelve Steps." Alcoholics Anonymous, 2024. https://aa.org/the-twelve-steps.

West, Christopher. *Good News About Sex and Marriage Revised Edition.* Cincinnati, OH: Servant Books, 2004.

West, Christopher. *Theology of the Body Explained: A Commentary on John Paul II's "Man and Woman He Created Them."* Boston, MA: Pauline Books & Media, 2007.

West, Christopher. *Theology of the Body for Beginners.* West Chester, PA: Ascension Press, 2004.

www.ingramcontent.com/pod-product-compliance
Lightning Source LLC
Chambersburg PA
CBHW070026100426
42740CB00013B/2603

* 9 7 9 8 8 8 8 7 0 4 6 4 6 *